EQUIPPING THE SAINTS

A PRACTICAL STUDY OF EPHESIANS 4:11–16

BILL BAGENTS
CORY COLLINS

CYPRESS
PUBLICATIONS

EQUIPPING THE SAINTS
A Practical Study of Ephesians 4:11–16
Published by Cypress Publications—an Imprint of Heritage Christian
University Press
Copyright © 2007, 2019 by Bill Bagents and Cory Collins
Manufactured in the United States of America

Cataloging-in-Publication Data
Bagents, Bill (William Ronald), 1956—
Equipping the Saints: A Practical Study of Ephesians 4:11–16 / by Bill Ba-
gents and Cory Collins
p. cm.
Includes Scripture index.
ISBN 978-1-7320483-5-5 (pbk.)
1. Bible. N.T. Ephesians—Study and teaching. 2. Christian life—Churches of
Christ authors.
I. Collins, Cory H., 1955—. II. Title.
BS2695.5 .B27 2019 227.5007—dc20 2019-933599

Cover design by Brittany McGuire

For information:
Cypress Publications
3625 Helton Drive
PO Box HCU
Florence, AL 35630
www.hcu.edu

DEDICATION

One of the blessings of serving the Mars Hill Church of Christ together was the consistent encouragement of Basil and Margie Overton. They dedicated their lives to the Lord and His church and helped equip countless others for effective service. We continue to learn from the example they set during their lives.

We dedicate this book to the Overtons' memory.

CONTENTS

FOREWORD

If you have acquired a copy of *Equipping the Saints* in hopes of finding a "quick fix" to identifying, growing, or utilizing your spiritual gifts, keep looking—and good luck. However, if you have been long for a resource to help *you* identify, grow, and use your spiritual gifts, congratulations! I believe you have found it!

In this book, as its title suggests, Bill Bagents and Cory Collins lead us through a discussion of Ephesians 4:11–16 and share their collective insights and thoughts regarding how each of us can recognize and utilize the gifts that have been given to us. Bill and Cory also help us understand that these gifts have not been given solely for our own personal advantage, but in order to build up and encourage the local, as well as universal body of Christ—His church.

Both of these men exemplify Christian servanthood combined with strength of character, command of the Scriptures, and genuine humility. For those of us who have been privileged to know Bill and Cory personally, we recognize that these men are themselves "equipped for every good work" and are thus uniquely qualified to lead this discussion and help church leaders and members alike access practical tools for recognizing and utilizing the gifts and talents God has given to each of us.

I first met Cory back in the mid-1970s when our undergraduate studies overlapped at David Lipscomb College (now Lipscomb University) in Nashville, Tennessee. He was a graduating senior, and I was an incoming freshman. Even then, you could tell that there was something special about Cory. His desire to serve God and God's people was apparent and obviously genuine to even those with just limited contact with him. Our paths went in different directions, but eventually came back together in 2000 when Cory came to serve as the pulpit minister for the Sherrod Avenue Church of Christ in Florence, Alabama. As one of the shepherds for the congregation, I was able to spend many hours working and praying with this humble and godly man. From the beginning of their work at Sherrod Avenue, Cory, his wife, Tanya, and their children, Christopher and Charissa, embraced and served members of the congregation and those in the surrounding community.

My acquaintance with Bill began in the early 2000s. Our sons competed with each other in track and field, and I knew him as a preacher for one of the other congregations in Florence. Later, I got to know Bill better, as he and my wife, Rosemary, worked together as family counselors for a Bible-based counselling center. One of the things that has drawn me to Bill is his unique and engaging wit. Additionally, he has a special way of analyzing a situation and describing it in common (and sometimes humorous) terms. I came to appreciate Bill even more when he became one of my professors and served as my advisor in the Master of Ministry program at Heritage Christian University.

I'm sure that either Bill or Cory individually could have written a book on this topic that would have provided readers with a great resource. The fact that they have collaborated in writing this book gives us the benefit of their combined knowledge and expertise. Knowing Bill and Cory as models of humility, I was struck early on in my reading by their focus on this important trait. As they argue, only a humble individual will recognize his or her need for help. Only a humble person will desire guidance from God's word. As I continued through *Equipping the Saints*, I found myself making notes for my own personal use, as well as for utilizing this material as a teaching resource. I was glad to see Bill and Cory sharing ideas that we have been incorporating into ministries at Sherrod Avenue. It's always nice to get confirmation from such quality people. I was also happy to get some new ideas that we could integrate into what we were already doing in order to do a better job of equipping our own members.

I believe you will find this book exceedingly useful in helping you be better equipped for more effective service; not only for personal growth, but also in helping to lead others (and we are all leaders to someone). The format of this book allows for personal study, for formal Bible class use, and for small group discussions.

May your life be blessed as you read *Equipping the Saints* and as you utilize the ideas that Bill and Cory have shared with us. Moreover, may God be glorified as you and your congregation are built up in love.

Don Snodgrass
Florence, Alabama
June 2019

INTRODUCTION

The Lord is the source of and the power behind all that is good (Jam 1:17). This is especially true of revival within His church. Spiritual revival flows from God and His word. Spiritual revival stirs a heightened appreciation of God's grace and a renewed zeal for good works (Titus 2:11–14). Spiritual revival calls us to repentance and godly living. Spiritual revival moves us to more fervent prayer, more joyous worship, and more complete dependence on God.

What are we saying? Spiritual revival has content; it has substance. Though it involves both, it's not just words and it's not just feelings. Revival which flows from God and His word changes lives. It changes hearts. It changes destinies. And, it changes behavior. Revival puts us right with God. Revival puts us to work for God. Revival challenges us to ask God to equip us to serve Him in His church. That is a prayer which certainly honors the Lord and which He is sure to hear favorably.

We live in an age when "work" is often viewed in a negative light. This is particularly true in the context of religion. Ephesians 2:8–9 is so often quoted, "For by grace you have been saved through faith, and that not of yourselves; it is the gift of God, not of works, lest anyone should boast." We can't save ourselves. We can't work our way to heaven. God saves us in Christ by grace through faith. Frequently some therefore treat work as unimportant or optional.

As true as Ephesians 2:8–9 is, Ephesians 2:10 is just as true. "For we are His workmanship, created in Christ Jesus for good works, which God prepared beforehand that we should walk in them." We who obey the gospel and are made alive by God are raised up together in Christ. We are raised to a new life, to a new hope, and to a new mission. As God's workmanship, we are God's workers. Ephesians 2:10 speaks of good works as an essential part of our daily walk with Christ.

Ephesians 4:1–16, the text from which this series of lessons is drawn, further describes that daily walk with Jesus. It reminds us that one key purpose of leadership within the church is "the equipping of the saints for the work of ministry for the edifying of the body of Christ." Thus, the purposes of these lessons are:

- To remind God's people of God's call to the work of ministry
- To remind God's leaders of God's call to equip the saints for the work of ministry
- To urge every Christian to become increasingly more equipped for the work of ministry

As the Lord revives, He also equips. He not only provides the energy for Christ-centered living; He supplies the tools for

Christ-centered ministry. We join the writer of Hebrews in offering this prayer: "Now the God of peace, who brought up from the dead the great Shepherd of the sheep through the blood of the eternal covenant, *even* Jesus our Lord, equip you in every good thing to do His will, working in us that which is pleasing in His sight, through Jesus Christ, to whom *be* the glory forever and ever. Amen" (Heb 13:20–21). The Greek term rendered here as "equip," καταρτίζω, also means "to put in order, restore, mend, or train." It describes the mending of nets, so that they may catch fish effectively (Matt 4:21; Mark 1:19). It appears again as Christians are taught to "be made complete" in the same mind and judgment (1 Cor 1:10). It emerges as Jesus speaks of His disciples being "fully trained" and becoming like their teacher (Luke 6:40).

The basis of that equipping is the Word of God itself. Because all Scripture is God-breathed, it is "profitable for teaching, for reproof, for correction, for training in righteousness; that the man of God may be adequate, equipped for every good work" (2 Tim 3:16–17). The Greek term used here, ἐξαρτίζω, also suggests "to fit, join, furnish, finish, or complete."

God equipped Noah with all he needed to accomplish his God-given task. God equipped Moses during his first forty years in Egypt, and his second forty years in Midian, for his third forty years involving the Passover, the Exodus, and the journey through the wilderness. God equipped David as a shepherd of sheep to become a shepherd of His people Israel (2 Sam 5:2; 7:8). God equipped the prophets, including Jeremiah, to whom He said, "Now behold, I have made you today as a fortified city, and as a pillar of iron and as walls of bronze against the whole land, to the kings of Judah, to its princes, to its priests and to the people of the land" (Jer 1:17–18). God equipped Esther, giving her the tools and opportunities she needed to appear before the king and deliver herself and her fellow Jews from annihilation. In each case there was a critical moment in which God's servant had to step up, accept God's equipment, and commit himself or herself to God's mission. Even abundant divine help would have gained nothing without genuine faith, courage, and resolve.

Furthermore, God used those whom He first equipped to equip still others. Moses equipped Joshua. David equipped Solomon. Elijah equipped Elisha. Paul equipped Timothy and Titus. May the lessons in this series encourage every reader to be equipped by God, according to His Word, through the leaders He has placed in the church. May these lessons urge every church leader to become God's tool for equipping all the saints for the work of ministry.

Please view these lessons as a work in progress. Use your knowledge of Scripture to supplement and improve each lesson. These brief lessons could hardly exhaust God's truth on their respective topics. Rearrange any lesson to fit your style of teaching and the needs of the class. Trust the power of God's word to change lives.

Bill Bagents
Cory Collins

EQUIPPING THE SAINTS

ONE
A TEACHABLE SPIRIT

Perhaps you've heard the old line, "You can always tell a man from Texas, but you can't tell him much." With apologies to Texans, we admit that geography has little to do with the truth of that line. There are people in every state and nation who lack the advantage of a teachable spirit. It takes a measure of humility to have that spirit.

We see the wonderful crafting of words in Ephesians 4:1–3 as one more evidence of the inspiration of Scripture (2 Tim 3:14–17). Paul first describes himself as "the prisoner of the Lord." He proceeds from that humble beginning to urge the Ephesians, and Christians of every age, to walk worthy of the gospel call (2 Thess 2:13–14). Part of that worthy walk is the attitude of "lowliness and gentleness." Paul's appeal is powerful because he has first set the example which he invites us to follow. He speaks as one who is submissive, unselfish, and has yielded himself. He writes, not as a domineering dictator, but as a surrendered slave. He does not demand; he beseeches or begs. From that subservient position and attitude he challenges us to lower ourselves, to be patient, and to bear with each other in love.

Of course Paul himself was following Christ. He urged us to do the same—to have "the mind of Christ." He wrote: "Let nothing be done through selfish ambition or conceit, but in lowliness of mind let each esteem others better than himself. Let each of you look out not only for his own interests, but also for the interests of others" (Phil 2:3–4). Then he noted that Jesus "emptied Himself," humbly denying Himself and taking on a servant's role in order to deliver us from sin.

According to Ephesians 4:1–3 all Christians have been called by God, though not all serve Him in the same capacity. Regardless of our age, gender, or ethnicity, we are among those God has summoned to walk worthy of His calling. Our word "vocation" comes from Latin. Meaning much more than "job" or "occupation," it originally referred to one's "calling." The idea is that, whatever our work, circumstances, or situation, we honor the Lord by giving our very best. Whatever we do, in word or deed, we are to "do it all in the name of the Lord Jesus, giving thanks through Him to God the Father" (Col 3:17).

The Greek term translated "worthy" means "of equal weight." None of us are worthy in the sense of deserving or earning a relationship with God. Jesus died for us when we were helpless and ungodly, sinners at enmity with God (Rom 5:6–11). However, in Christ, God has called us to live in a way that fits, that suits, that corresponds to His purposes for us. John puts it this way: "But if we walk in the light as He is in the light, we have fellowship with one another, and the blood of Jesus Christ His Son cleanses us from all sin" (1 John 1:7).

Humility fosters patience. It enables us to get along with one another. Humility supports unity. It enables us to see how much we need one another. And humility undergirds "the equipping of the saints for the work of ministry" (Eph 4:12). How so? We will consider answers from two important perspectives.

HUMILITY AND LEARNING

Without humility, there can be little willingness to learn. We say "little willingness" because it is possible that a selfish person could want to gain some specific skill, because it helps him get ahead. But we know this exception is beyond the context of Ephesians 4. Ephesians 4 deals with a specific type of equipping, "the equipping of the saints for the work of ministry." The saints are God's people, Christians. The work of ministry is God's work, work of service to God. Selfish people would hardly want to be equipped for selfless service.

Ephesians 4:11–16 presupposes a person who wants to be equipped to serve. This believer wants to encourage others. This Christian wants to grow up into the likeness of Christ. That rules out the person who thinks that he already has all the answers. It rules out the person who thinks that he has arrived or that he is good enough. It presupposes a person who wants to grow and is willing to learn from godly leaders. It presupposes a person who truly loves God.

Only a humble person could welcome training for service. Only a humble person could see himself as needing the help and guidance of spiritual leaders. In fact, only a humble person could want and welcome the guidance of God's word (Psa 119:105; 1 Pet 2:2–3).

Jesus prayed these remarkable words: "I thank You, Father, Lord of heaven and earth, that You have hidden these things from the wise and prudent and revealed them to babes. Even so, Father, for so it seemed good in Your sight" (Luke 10:21). Surely the "babes" are those able to see, understand, and grasp the things of God because their humble hearts are receptive to His teaching. The "wise and prudent" must be those who are such in their own estimation, foolishly thinking that they have all the answers already.

When the disciples came to Jesus, saying, "Who then is greatest in the kingdom of heaven?" Jesus called a little child to Him, set him in the midst of them, and said, "Assuredly, I say to you, unless you are converted and become as little children, you will by no means enter the kingdom of heaven. Therefore whoever humbles himself as this little child is the greatest in the kingdom of heaven" (Matt 18:1–4). Jesus also spoke of those "who have ears to hear" (Mark 4:9).

Teachers love students who want to learn. It's virtually impossible to teach those who lack the desire to learn. It's just as difficult for even the godliest leaders to teach (equip) those who do not want to grow in their service to Christ. Without humility, we're just not teachable. Without humility, we won't have either the desire or the ability to be equipped for ministry.

James wrote by inspiration, "God resists the proud but gives grace to the humble. Therefore submit to God. Resist the devil and he will flee from you. Draw near to God and He will draw near to you. Cleanse your hands, you sinners; and purify your hearts, you double-minded. Lament and mourn and weep! Let your laughter be turned to mourning and your joy to gloom. Humble yourselves in the sight of the Lord, and He will lift you up" (Jam 4:6–10). That "lifting up" suggests God's power to bless, equip, and restore those who humbly draw near to Him and lean on His strength.

HUMILITY AND TEACHING

God Himself blesses the church with leaders. One key reason that He does so is so that these leaders can equip the saints for the work of ministry. What kind of leader is most able to equip another Christian for service?

One answer focuses on ability. The leader who is most able to equip another person is the one who has and uses the skill in question. We could say it like this: those who are equipped can best equip others. That's common sense. It reminds Christian leaders to be sure that they never "retire" from God's service. It encourages Christian leaders to keep growing in their ability to serve.

Another answer focuses on attitude. The leader who is most able to equip another person to share in the ministry of Christ is the one who shows the sweet spirit of Christ. To put it another way, leaders who show humility, gentleness, and patience are most able to help others learn to serve.

Scripture teaches that "a servant of the Lord must not quarrel but be gentle to all, able to teach, patient, in humility correcting those who are in opposition, if God perhaps will grant them repentance, so that they may know the truth, and that they may come to their senses and escape the snare of the devil, having been taken captive by him to do his will" (2 Tim 2:22–26). See also 1 Timothy 4:11–16.

We know that it's possible to learn or develop skills from a teacher who has a bad attitude. We also know how difficult and unpleasant that is. Humility is the oil that lubricates the teaching process. Humility provides the background, the atmosphere, and the approach required for effective teaching. After all, if the teacher humbles himself or herself, how much easier it should be for the students to do the same. Jesus made this very point when He washed His disciples' feet. He said, "You call Me Teacher and Lord, and you say well, for so I am. If I then, your Lord and Teacher, have washed your feet, you also ought to wash one another's feet" (John 13:13–14). He also asked on that occasion, "For who is greater, he who sits at the table, or he who serves? Is it not he who sits at the table? Yet I am among you as the One who serves" (Luke 22:27).

When all of us have the teachable spirit noted here, we will in fact be "maintaining the unity of the Spirit in the bond of peace." A shared sense of calling, a desire to walk worthily, and a gentle, forbearing, loving commitment to God and each other are vital to the securing and strengthening of the ties that bind us together.

The equipping discussed in Ephesians 4:1–16 has to do with far more than just facts and skills. It has to do with the work, the character, and the attitude of Christ. Only a person who truly knows Jesus can effectively equip others in the way that Paul is describing here.

DISCUSSION QUESTIONS

1. How can a good teacher balance humility with the need to project an image of conviction and competence in what he or she teaches?

2. Today, there are no apostles or prophets living among us. Does this make the church less able to equip us for God's work?

3. Describe the Christian who is most able (best prepared) to be equipped for the work of ministry. List and discuss key characteristics of this person.

4. How could a Christian leader "check his attitude" to be sure that it best enables him to equip others for service?

5. Besides a lack of humility, what could keep Christians from wanting to be equipped to share in the work of Christ?

6. Can one overdo "humility" to the point that he never feels qualified to teach? Consider James 3:1ff.

7. On what occasions in Jesus' ministry do you see Him demonstrating humility?

8. Why is it so crucial that we, as learners and as teachers, "walk the walk" rather than merely "talking the talk"?

TWO
AN INFORMED MIND

It has often been said that Christianity is a taught religion. Jesus came as a teacher, sent from God (John 3:2). He Himself declared, "It is written in the prophets, 'And they shall all be taught of God.' Everyone who has heard and learned from the Father, comes to Me" (John 6:45). Jude's famous phrase, "the faith which was once for all delivered to the saints," speaks of a body of doctrine, a body of truth, which God has revealed (Jude 3). This in no way speaks against the importance of knowing Christ Himself personally or of having a right relationship with God (Phil 3:8–11; Rom 5:1–11). It is simply a reminder that virtually everything we know about God and His will we know from Scripture.

MINISTRY AND DOCTRINE

Sadly, some people seem to believe that "doctrine" is a divisive word. Some have made statements like, "We just need to love and help people like Jesus did. It is love, not doctrine,

11

that identifies real Christians." Truly, Jesus identified love as one key way that the world would know His disciples (John 13:34–35). But biblical love, like biblical faith, has content (1 Cor 13). Both are based in the truth of God's revelation. It is inevitable that while some will accept the doctrine, some will distort it, and some will reject it. Jesus said, "He who has ears to hear, let him hear" (Matt 11:15). Paul predicted, speaking to the elders from Ephesus, that "from among your own selves men will arise, speaking perverse things, to draw away the disciples after them" (Acts 20:30). Peter, noting that there are "some things hard to understand" in Scripture, said that "the untaught and unstable" would distort God's pure doctrine, "to their own destruction" (2 Pet 3:16).

The idea that we can please God by serving and encouraging others—regardless of what doctrine we may believe—is false! In our better moments, we know this by common sense. "Doctrine" is teaching. For example, the teaching that Jesus is "the Christ, the Son of the living God," is doctrine (Matt 16:16). In light of John 8:24, it is the kind of doctrine which is essential to salvation. Scripture never sets love and obedience at odds. Jesus said both, "If you love Me, you will keep My commandments" (John 14:15), and, "You are My friends, if you do what I command you" (John 15:14). Scripture never sets doctrine and service at odds. It was Jesus, the "Teacher and Lord," who instructed His disciples to serve by washing their feet (John 13:12–15). The Lord wants His people to love Him, believe Him, obey Him, and serve Him.

Ephesians 4:4–6 gives an essential doctrinal foundation for understanding the remainder of that great chapter. Paul again points out that all Christians are called; compare Ephesians 4:1 with Ephesians 4:3. Then he lists seven absolute, unchanging "ones" involved in our calling.

There is one body, and that body is the church. Ephesians 1:22–23 indicates that the Father "put all things in subjection under His feet, and gave Him as head over all things to the church, which is His body, the fullness of Him who fills all in all." The Lord adds the saved to that body (Acts 2:40–47). We all enter the body the same way: "For by one Spirit we were all baptized into one body, whether Jews or Greeks, whether slaves or free, and we were all made to drink of one Spirit" (1 Cor 12:13).

There is one Spirit. The passage just cited indicates that we were baptized "by one Spirit" and that we were made to drink of "one Spirit." That same Holy Spirit inspired every word of Scripture (2 Tim 3:16–17; 2 Pet 1:19–21). He personally dwells within each Christian (Rom 8:9–11).

The one hope of our calling is the one hope of the gospel, everlasting salvation with God in heaven (1 Cor15). It is no mere wish, fantasy, or dream. It is a matter of certain, confident expectation (Phil 1:20). One whose hope is in the Lord will never be disappointed or put to shame (Rom 9:33; 10:11.) We share "in the hope of eternal life, which God, who cannot lie, promised long ages ago" (Titus 1:2).

Jesus Christ is our one Lord. The Scripture says, "For even if there are so-called gods whether in heaven or on earth, as indeed there are many gods and many lords, yet for us there is but one God, the Father, from whom are all things, and we exist for Him; and one Lord, Jesus Christ, by whom are all things, and we exist through Him" (1 Cor 8:5–6). No one can serve two masters (Matt 6:24). One who calls Jesus "Lord" must do as He says (Luke 6:46).

Faith in Him is our one faith, "the faith once delivered" (Jude 3). People kept hearing about Paul, "He who once persecuted us is now preaching the faith which he once tried to destroy" (Gal 1:23). And faith in Him includes believing every truth of God's word (Matt 19:16–22; John 12:42–50).

The one baptism is baptism into Christ for the remission of sins (Acts 2:37–38; Gal 3:26–27). It is the baptism which Jesus commanded in the Great Commission, the significance and validity of which would continue until the end of the age (Matt 28:18–20).

The magnificence of God the Father is the very beginning point of all truth (Gen 1:1). "God" suggests His sovereignty, power, and immortality; "Father" suggests His tenderness, His love, and His approachability. Romans 11:36 states, "For from Him and through Him and to Him are all things. To Him be the glory forever. Amen."

MINISTRY AND THE CHURCH

Sadly, some people seem to believe that even the concept of "church" is divisive. Some have made statements like, "I love Jesus, but I have no need for organized religion. I'll just serve Him on my own and leave church to those who need it. I have my own ministry." It is true that there is far more to genuine Christianity than just "attending church." At the same time,

Ephesians is a church letter. Notice how "body language" permeates chapter four.

Perhaps some mistakenly think of the church as an organization rather than an organism, as a building rather than a body, or as a corporation rather than a community. However, anyone who loves Jesus and sees the church as an extension of Jesus will love the church. One cannot truly love the groom and despise the bride whom the groom loves. One cannot respect the head and minimize the value of the body which the head leads.

The "Seven Ones" of Ephesians 4:4–6 are foundational truths of biblical doctrine. That list of foundational truths begins with the one body. There is one body, and, as noted above, Scripture identifies that body as the church (Eph 5:22–33; Col 1:18). A key reason that God puts leaders in the church is so that those leaders can equip the saints for the work of ministry (Eph 4:11–12). One goal of this equipping is "the edifying [encouragement, building up] of the body of Christ" (Eph 4:12). This encouragement leads to greater knowledge and faith. Growing in knowledge and faith leads Christians to become even more like Jesus (Eph 4:13–15). And becoming more like Jesus even more strongly unites the body (Eph 4:16).

To put it another way, unity is a theme in Ephesians 4. Christians are to have the attitudes that build unity (4:1–3). We are to believe the foundational truths which are essential to unity (4:4–6). We are to become equipped for the work of ministry so that we can encourage one another to grow more like Jesus, which also builds unity (4:12–16).

Perhaps we should ask the obvious question: "Builds the unity of what?" Sound doctrine and faithful ministry build the unity of the church. Both Christian unity and Christian ministry must be grounded in the truth of God. When they are, the body grows, and each individual member becomes more like Jesus. In other words, the church lives out the doctrine of Christ so that others may see Christ in each of us and in all of us.

The goal or result of faithful ministry is that God is seen to be "over all and through all and in all" in everything that pertains to the church. The church is the microcosm, or miniature world in itself, in which God is fully magnified. Seen in that light, ministry and church leadership take on a wonderful, immeasurable significance. Because of that, every follower of Christ should eagerly seek to serve and to lead, according to God's gracious will.

Think of ways in which the factors in Ephesians 4:1–6 build upon each other in an escalating cycle. A sense of God's high calling causes us to want to walk in a worthy manner. We begin that walk with humility, gentleness, patience, forbearance, and love. We exert our maximum effort to maintain God-given, Bible-based unity, along with harmonious peace. We find a new appreciation for the seven absolutes of unity, and we highly cherish each one. Therefore, we become even more aware of our heavenly calling, more determined to walk in a worthy manner, and so forth. The cycle continues without end.

Imagine a church in which every person is caught up in the same desire, the same direction, and the same determination described in Ephesians 4:1-6. In such a setting, biblical doctrine will be upheld without compromise; biblical leadership will empower and equip Christ-like ministry in ways otherwise impossible; and biblical church growth will be evident in every way that pleases God.

DISCUSSION QUESTIONS

1. If a person is doing great works for God, does it really matter what doctrine he or she believes? How does Matthew 7:21-23 impact your answer? What about Acts 10:1-8 and Revelation 3:14-22?

2. Does the Lord expect Christians to be united? If so, in what sense? On what basis?

3. Is it accurate to say, "Ephesians is a church letter"? How do you know?

4. Why might some claim that church is irrelevant to authentic Christian ministry?

5. Why might some see no strong connection between sound doctrine and authentic Christian ministry?

6. Which teachings [doctrines] of Scripture do you see as the most powerful encouragement to Christian ministry?

7. What difference does it make to have God alone as the center and focus of ministry?

8. How do the elements and ideas in Ephesians 4:1–6 supplement and strengthen each other?

THREE
GOD'S GRACE

There are senses in which the general or common grace of God has been extended to every person, whether Christian or not. Jesus referred to the sunshine and the rain as God's gifts to all people, good or evil (Matt 5:45). Paul told the pagan crowd at Lystra that God "did not leave Himself without witness, in that He did good and gave you rains from heaven and fruitful seasons, satisfying your hearts with food and gladness" (Acts 14:17). Paul told the idolatrous philosophers of Athens, "For in Him [the one true God] we live and move and have our being" (Acts 17:28). God's revealed word is an extension of His grace. The preaching of the gospel is a universal offer of God's saving grace.

In Ephesians 4:7, Paul speaks more specifically of grace. He speaks of the grace which has been given to every obedient believer "according to the measure of Christ's gift." Because Jesus died for us and we live in Christ, we know the tremendous blessing of the forgiveness of sins. Salvation is the greatest of Christ's gifts. But this great text is teaching us that and more. In addition to the gift of eternal life, Jesus has provided individual gifts, strengths, and skills to implement the church's growth and maturity.

These gifts are possible only because of Jesus' ascension. Jesus Christ, after descending from heaven to earth, ascended far above all others, led His captives to victory, and gave these blessings to men. Paul quotes from Psalm 68, well worth reading in its entirety. There David saw God ascending a high mountain, reminiscent of Mount Sinai. In doing so He took captives in His procession and won spoils from His enemies that He then shared with His subjects.

The New Testament draws powerful implications from the ascension of Christ. Because He ascended, we can be sure that He will return in like manner (Acts 1:9–11). We also know that in the ascension He took His place beside the Father. Peter proclaimed on Pentecost, "Therefore being exalted to the right hand of God, and having received from the Father the promise of the Holy Spirit, He poured out this which you now see and hear. For David did not ascend into the heavens, but he says himself: 'The LORD said to my Lord, "Sit at My right hand, till I make Your enemies Your footstool." ' Therefore let all the house of Israel know assuredly that God has made this Jesus, whom you crucified, both Lord and Christ" (Acts 2:33–36).

MANIFESTATIONS OF GOD'S GRACE

One function of Ephesians 4:7-10 is to set the stage for the next section (verses 11–16) of Paul's letter. One manifestation of God's grace is the spiritual leadership provided by godly men. Other manifestations of God's grace which are discussed in Ephesians 4 include the following:

- The potential for every Christian to become equipped for the work of ministry;
- The potential for every Christian to edify the body of Christ;
- The potential for every Christian to grow into maturity in Christ;
- And the potential for every Christian to help cause the growth of the body.

Only Jesus Christ could offer such tremendous opportunity. Only Jesus Christ could bring about such an amazing change in people.

It is marvelous to see how Jesus did just that in the life of Simon Peter. He took a brash, impulsive, rough, sometimes frightened fisherman, and He called him "rock" (Cephas or Peter). He made him his spokesman on the Day of Pentecost. He gave this coward amazing courage. Though Peter had once denied Jesus even before a servant girl, he confessed Jesus boldly before the authorities in Acts 4 and 5. With the other apostles he answered and said, "We must obey God rather than men" (Acts 5:29–32). Others could see the change Jesus made as well. Luke writes, "Now as they observed the confidence of Peter and John, and understood that they were uneducated and untrained men, they were marveling, and began to recognize them as having been with Jesus" (Acts 4:13).

The entire letter to the Ephesians strongly elevates Jesus Christ as the source of salvation and as the greatest manifestation of God's grace. Ephesians 1:3 blesses God the Father "who has blessed us with every spiritual blessing in the heavenly places in Christ." Notice how many times the phrase "in Christ" is found in Ephesians. Read the tremendous words of praise and encouragement which end chapter 3 (Eph 3:20–21). The Lord Himself is the power behind the work of the church. The Lord Himself is the power behind every worker within His church. Paul says this of himself and his ministry in Ephesians 3:1–7.

Implications for Every Christian

Perhaps the first implication which should be considered is that the words of Ephesians are words for Christians, all Christians. Christians are the "each one of us" to whom grace has been given according to the measure of Christ's gift (4:7). No one who is in Christ is excluded. Christians are the saints who need to be equipped for the work of ministry (4:12). Christians are those who are in Christ and who can "grow up in all things into Him who is the head—Christ" (4:15). None of these blessings is available outside Christ.

A second implication is that the equipping of Christians for the work of ministry is not simply a human endeavor. The process of equipping and the work of ministry itself are part of God's plan. Both are based in God's truth and God's grace.

As we grow in our ability to serve God, we are growing in Christ. We do this with God's blessing and with God's help.

Perhaps a third implication is found in Ephesians 4:4, which is a quotation of Psalm 68:18. While the greatest gift of Christ is salvation, salvation is not His only gift. Often, we think of gifts in terms of talents or abilities. In that light, what other gifts has He given His disciples? A popular modern answer says, "God gives each of His people a special gift for ministry. What we need to do is to find our gift and put it to work for God." We recognize our every ability as a gift from God. We readily admit that God has blessed some Christians with special abilities. Some sing wonderfully. Others teach or preach powerfully. Some have a special way with children or with the elderly.

The Word of God provides several lists of various, non-miraculous, gifts which God has given His people. Peter writes, "As each one has received a special gift, employ it in serving one another, as good stewards of the manifold grace of God. Whoever speaks, let him speak, as it were, the utterances of God; whoever serves, let him do so as by the strength which God supplies; so that in all things God may be glorified through Jesus Christ, to whom belongs the glory and dominion forever and ever. Amen" (1 Pet 4:10–11).

"Manifold" suggests many-sided, multi-faceted, as the numerous angles seen in a beautifully-cut diamond. As the same water may be poured into unique and different containers, so the grace of God takes on different forms and expressions. Some may speak; others may serve. Each is to do what he does as a steward, managing a gift which actually belongs to another.

Paul writes in Romans 12:6–8, "And since we have gifts that differ according to the grace given to us, let each exercise them accordingly: if prophecy, according to the proportion of his faith; if service, in his serving; or he who teaches, in his teaching; or he who exhorts, in his exhortation; he who gives, with liberality; he who leads, with diligence; he who shows mercy, with cheerfulness."

Having noted the presence of individual gifts, we believe that a word of caution is in order. Scripture never says that the Lord gives only one gift or even one "ministry" to each Christian. "The work of ministry" for which the saints are to be equipped is a broad, far-reaching phrase. As will be explored in Lesson 5, the work of ministry includes many godly activities in which every Christian must share. Not only that, but there is the great principle taught in the Parable of the Talents (Matt 25:14–30). While the "talents" in that parable refer to a weight of gold or silver, we believe the principle applies more broadly. What would we do with a great king's money that he entrusted to our care? We will do the same with every blessing or gift which the heavenly King has given us. We must say with Paul, "Let a man regard us in this manner, as servants of Christ, and stewards of the mysteries of God. In this case, moreover, it is required of stewards that one be found trustworthy" (1 Cor 4:1–2). Those who are faithful in God's service will be blessed with even greater opportunity to serve (Matt 25:21, 23). God can expand even our abilities to serve.

The gift of one special ability should not limit our service to God. Special aptitude for one aspect of ministry need not lead us to neglect other important avenues of service. Obviously, Jesus Himself demonstrated a multitude of gifts as a man in His earthly ministry. As we learn to imitate Him, we seek to be strong in all the areas in which He was strong. The New Testament repeatedly urges us to have the mind of Christ (Phil 2:1-11), to walk in His steps (1 Pet 2:21–25; 1 John 2:6), and even to run with perseverance the race which He has already completed (Heb 12:1–3) Paul notes that God predestined us "to become conformed to the image of His Son, that He might be the first-born among many brethren" (Rom 8:29).

And nothing says that Christ gives us all His gifts at once. Ephesians 4 strongly implies that some of those gifts may be gained as we learn to be more like Jesus. Surely maturity and growth involve using what gifts we already have more effectively, as well as acquiring and developing other gifts that will aid us in faithfully reflecting the image of Christ.

DISCUSSION QUESTIONS

1. How will viewing our abilities as gifts from God affect our use of those talents?

2. How might a greater emphasis on Christ's ascension enhance our service to Him?

3. Read and outline Psalm 68. What does it reveal about God? About His purpose? About our role?

4. Why might it be tempting for some to limit God's power by describing themselves as having only one gift or talent?

5. Is it really true that God can expand our abilities to serve? Support your answer.

6. Specifically how might God expand a person's ability to serve Him?

7. What can we do to invite God to give us greater ability and opportunity to serve?

8. In what specific area(s) do you seek to become more like Christ?

FOUR
LEADERS TRAINING WORKERS

"**A**nd He gave." Repeatedly Scripture affirms that the roles, positions, and skills of leaders are granted to them by the grace of God. For that reason there is no ground for boasting or rivalry. Leaders are not territorial; whatever turf they occupy is not their own but the Lord's. Paul warned the Corinthians "that no one of you might become arrogant in behalf of one against the other. For who regards you as superior? And what do you have that you did not receive? But if you did receive it, why do you boast as if you had not received it?" (1 Cor 4:6–7)

Rather than comparing or competing, Christ-like leaders cooperate. Paul insisted, "For we are not bold to class or compare ourselves with some of those who commend themselves; but when they measure themselves by themselves, and compare themselves with themselves, they are without understanding. But we will not boast beyond our measure, but within the measure of the sphere which God apportioned to us as a measure, to reach even as far as you"

(2 Cor 10:12–13). Grateful and content in the sphere in which God has placed each person, that person is free to help others serve effectively in their own spheres, without pride or jealousy.

Some of the leadership roles listed in Ephesians 4:11 were of limited duration. To be an apostle one must have accompanied Jesus from the time of His baptism and have been an eyewitness of the resurrected Christ (Acts 1:21–22). We recognize Paul as an exception, as "one born out of due season;" but even he was an eyewitness of the resurrected Lord (Acts 26:12–18; 1 Cor 15:1–11). The prophetic ministry was limited to the time of miraculous spiritual gifts (1 Cor 13:8–13). Though these leadership gifts did not continue, they served the same purpose as the leadership gifts which do remain. They equipped the saints for ministry.

The leadership roles of evangelists, pastors, and teachers are ongoing blessings from God. It may be of interest to note that many see "pastors and teachers" as a single role, reflecting the "teaching elder" described in 1 Timothy 5:17. Whether two or three lasting leadership roles are being described, a key purpose of spiritual leadership is emphasized in our text. The Lord enables leaders "for the equipping of the saints for the work of ministry."

FROM THE BEGINNING

Christianity has never been a spectator religion. Even in His earthly ministry, Jesus involved His followers in God's work. When He called twelve, He empowered them for ministry and sent them out to preach the gospel (Matt 10). Luke 10 reminds us that even the great work of preaching the gospel was not limited just to Jesus and the twelve. When the Lord fed the 5,000, the apostles served (Matt 15). In fact, Jesus taught that it was service that defines greatness in His kingdom (Matt 20:20–28). It was service that defined Jesus' own ministry, "just as the Son of Man did not come to be served, but to serve, and to give His life a ransom for many." Being involved in the work of ministry is an essential part of following the example of Jesus.

It was to all His followers that Jesus said, "If anyone wishes to come after Me, let him deny himself, and take up his cross daily, and follow Me" (Luke 9:23). Then He added, "No one, after putting his hand to the plow and looking back, is fit for the kingdom of God" (Luke 9:62). Calling everyone to ministry in the sense of service, Jesus said: "but whoever wishes to become great among you shall be your servant; and whoever wishes to be first among you shall be slave of all. For even the Son of Man did not come to be served, but to serve, and to give His life a ransom for many" (Mark 10:43–45).

It has been said often, "Give a man a fish, and he will eat for a day. Teach that man to fish, and he will eat for a lifetime." In addition that man will feed many others who are dependent upon him. As he then teaches them to fish, he continues the process and multiplies the product. Long ago, as Jesus was going along by the Sea of Galilee, "He saw Simon and Andrew, the brother of Simon, casting a net in the sea; for they were fishermen. And Jesus said to them, 'Follow Me, and I will make you become fishers of men'" (Mark 1:16–17).

An anonymous source has stated: "Tell me and I forget; show me and I remember; involve me and I understand." One may also say, "Involve me and I will become more interested and want to be even more involved." Interest and involvement increase together, each contributing to the other in a wonderful upward spiral. The same is true of faith and works. Faith leads a believer to work; that work in turn builds and increases the believer's faith.

The first Christians understood the truth of Jesus' teaching. Those converted on the Pentecost following Christ's resurrection, "sold their possessions and goods, and divided them among all, as anyone had need" (Acts 2:45). They opened their hearts and their homes to one another (Acts 2:46–47; 4:32–37). The disciple, Tabitha, is described as a woman "full of good works and charitable deeds" (Acts 9:36). Could it be that her faithful service led the Lord to allow Peter to raise her from the dead? Paul praised the Philippians for their works of service (Phil 4:10–20). To each of the seven churches of Asia, Jesus said, "I know your works..." (Rev 2–3). He knew their good works, and He knew the areas in which their work was slack.

The New Testament repeatedly urges Christians to be involved in God's work. The great resurrection chapter concludes, "Therefore, my beloved brethren, be steadfast, immovable, always abounding in the work of the Lord, knowing that your labor is not in vain in the Lord" (1 Cor 15:58). Paul reminded the Colossians that every word or deed in the Christian's life is to be done in the name of the Lord Jesus, "giving thanks through Him to God the Father " (Col 3:17). Even our attitude toward "everyday work" has been changed by the fact that we "serve the Lord Christ" (Col 3:22–24). In his letter to Titus, Paul repeatedly emphasized the importance of good works (Titus 2:6–8, 11–14; 3:1, 8, and 14). From the beginning of the church, God has expected His people to be involved in the work of ministry.

IMPLICATIONS FOR LEADERS AND FOLLOWERS

Spiritual leaders purposefully work to equip the saints for the work of ministry. They know that this is God's will. They know that involved people are happy people. They know that involved people are growing people. They also know that the Jesus' church, as great as it is, has little to offer those who "just come and sit."

How do spiritual leaders work to equip the saints for the work of ministry? They pray for God's wisdom and guidance (Jam 1:5). They search the Scriptures for examples of equipping. They teach the facts, attitudes, and skills which equip the saints. They may even schedule special equipping classes. They mentor younger disciples, like Paul mentored Timothy and Titus. They work to provide the maximum opportunity for every Christian to be involved in ministry. And they continually encourage the brethren.

The military term "point man" refers to the soldier who stands at the point position, in front of the other troops. He takes the primary risks upon himself by going first across a field that may be laced with land mines. His courage, vision, and action become the model which those behind him imitate.

If he hits a mine, it is he alone and not the whole company that suffers. If he arrives safely, the others must simply think as he thinks and move as he moves in order to join him on the other side.

One thinks first of Jesus Himself as the point man who first ran the race and tasted death for every man (Heb 12:1–3; 2:9). Secondly, each leader in the church is a point man. Each leader must know the way, go the way, and show the way. He charts the course and stays the course, and he beckons others to come behind him. As Paul said, so each leader says, "Be imitators of me, just as I also am of Christ" (1 Cor 11:1).

Now let us think of the other side of the coin. How do disciples of Christ help their spiritual leaders in the work of equipping? We, too, pray for God's wisdom and guidance. We, too, keep learning from God's word. We actively seek ways to serve, being constantly aware of the needs of others (Rom 12:9–21; Gal 6:1–5; Phil 2:3–4; Jam 2:14–17; 1 John 3:16–18). We keep the ready, willing, and able mindset of Titus 2:11–3:2. We consistently choose to encourage our brethren by including and involving them in our work for God.

Hebrews 13:17 makes it apparent that followers have much to contribute to the effectiveness and continued eagerness of their leaders. It states: "Obey your leaders and submit to them; for they keep watch over your souls, as those who will give an account. Let them do this with joy and not with grief, for this would be unprofitable for you." We easily see the benefit of leaders who are joyful rather than grieved. They are a pleasure to follow. When we obey and submit to them, we become a pleasure to lead. Leaders quit perhaps because of discouragement more than any other reason. Let us who follow determine to make our leaders glad every day that they took on such serious responsibilities for the Lord and for us.

If we need more help, we share that with the elders and with other older brethren. We specifically ask them to help us learn how to serve the Lord better. We don't wait until we are asked to do what the Bible tells us to do. We refuse just to sit and watch.

Discussion Questions

1. In that there are no apostles or prophets living among us today, is the church still able to equip the saints for the work of ministry? Explain.

2. Why did Jesus so fully involve His disciples in the work of His ministry?

3. Why might some leaders be tempted to limit the involvement of other Christians?

4. Whether intentional or not, how might some leaders limit the involvement of other Christians?

5. What are the greatest dangers that will be faced by a congregation which does not work to equip and involve every member?

6. What will be the blessings of a congregation that does the work of equipping?

7. What attitudes and traits are most important for followers to have?

FIVE
A BIBLICAL UNDERSTANDING

As we read Ephesians 4:11–16, a natural question is, "What is the work of ministry?" Some have a very narrow view of ministry. They think only of leading in the public worship of the church. Because much of the religious world observes a distinction between clergy and laity, others think only of the work usually done by a preacher. This may include preaching, and assisting with weddings, funerals, baptisms, and the like. The Bible, however, takes a much broader view of ministry.

The New Testament never teaches the concept of a clergy/laity distinction. On the contrary, God's word affirms the priesthood of every believer. All of us are to "offer up spiritual sacrifices acceptable to God through Jesus Christ" (1 Pet 2:5, 9–10). Every Christian can offer the sacrifice of praise to God (Heb 13:15–16). In fact, every Christian offers himself, his own body, as a living sacrifice to God (Rom 12:1–2). Every Christian can approach God directly in prayer (Heb 4:14–16; 1 Thess 5:16–22). Every Christian can encourage the church and contribute to the growth of the church (Eph 4:11–16). Hebrews 6:10 speaks of ministry in connection with all Christians: "For God is not unjust so as to forget your work and the love which you have shown toward His name, in having ministered and in still ministering to the saints."

GOD'S VIEW OF MINISTRY

In the New Testament, "minister" is not a term reserved for those who have been ordained. "Minister" means servant, and every Christian is a servant of God. "Ministry" is not a term reserved for special religious acts. Every good action which is done to the glory of God is ministry. This truth has led some to say, "True Christianity is ministry." True Christianity is a life of service to God and others. It is a life lived to the glory of God (Matt 5:13–16; 7:21–23).

To put it another way, the preacher is a minister who preaches; he is an evangelist, to use the term from Ephesians 4:11. The sister in the nursery is a minister who cares for others' children. The custodian is a minister who maintains the church's property. The elder is a minister who leads, over-sees, and shepherds the flock. Therefore, it can be misleading to refer only to the preacher as "the minister." That phraseology can create another misunderstanding. It can cause people to think that "the minister" is here to minister to us, rather than to equip us to minister to others. In this unbiblical scenario we are passive recipients of ministry rather than active participants in ministry.

While all Christians are to minister, church leaders minister by helping others minister. This is obvious from our text. The evangelists, pastors, and teachers are ministers who equip. The fruit of their work is seen in the growth of the work of others. They measure their own progress and faithfulness by the preparation, development, and maturation of the various members of the church in their respective roles. They do their part, but they also aid others in finding and doing theirs. While they do their share of visiting, for example, they are devoted to training and empowering others to visit. The same is true in every aspect of evangelism, edification, and benevolence.

This one concept, taken seriously and implemented effectively, will transform the church from an audience to an army, from watchers to workers, and from recipients to participants. Imagine a congregation in which literally every person contributes actively to its health and growth. There is no limit to what the Lord can do through such a body of His saints. Of course that is where Paul is headed when he says that the church, "the whole body, being fitted and held together by that which every joint supplies, according to the proper working of each individual part, causes the growth of the body for the building up of itself in love" (Eph 4:16).

What a concept: everyone working side by side, in harmony, under one Head, for one purpose. That picture reminds us of the emphasis upon unity with which Ephesians 4 (and our study) began. We start with a high sense of calling, a humble sense of self, and a holy sense of devotion. We therefore maintain the unity of the Spirit in the bond of peace and cling without wavering to the seven absolutes of oneness. Recognizing our gifts, and submitting to our leaders, we apply ourselves diligently to the life, health, and growth of the church in the image of Christ.

So, within the unity of focus there is diversity of function. Because the joints and parts function in their own unique and diverse ways, ministry encompasses all facets of the Lord's work. Jesus gives us great help in avoiding the temptation to think of ministry too narrowly. What qualifies as ministry in Jesus' view? Jesus said, "And whoever gives one of these little ones only a cup of cold water in the name of a disciple, assuredly, I say to you, he shall by no means lose his reward" (Matt 10:42). He recognized the poor widow who gave two coins which were worth only a fraction of a penny (Mark 12:41–44). He promised that the good deed of the woman who anointed Him with fragrant oil would be told "wherever the gospel is preached in the whole world" (Mark 14:3–9).

The judgment scene of Matthew 25:31–46 deserves special attention. We know that even this long passage does not give every criterion by which we will be judged (See Matt 12:33–37, 2 Cor 5:9–11, and Rev 20:11–15). Still, the criteria given here are fascinating. Those who are saved are blessed for having fed the hungry, given drink to the thirsty, showed hospitality to the stranger, clothed the naked, and visited the sick and imprisoned. Whenever they served even "one of the least of these My brethren," Jesus said, "You did it to me" (Matt 25:40). The very opposite is said of those who are sent away into everlasting punishment. It is clear that Jesus has a very broad and practical view of ministry.

OUR UNDERSTANDING OF MINISTRY

In keeping with Ephesians 4:11–16, it is accurate to say that "the work of ministry" includes any action which encourages (edifies) the body of Christ. It encompasses all actions which contribute to the unity and growth of the body. What categories and behaviors might this idea involve? Consider the following partial list:

- *Participating joyfully in worship.* "Speaking to one another in psalms and hymns and spiritual songs, singing and making melody with your heart to the Lord" (Eph 5:19) See also Colossians 3:16; Hebrews 10:19–25.

- *Praying for one another.* "Devote yourselves to prayer, keeping alert in it with an attitude of thanksgiving; praying at the same time for us as well, that God may open up to us a door for the word, so that we may speak forth the mystery of Christ, for which I have also been imprisoned; in order that I may make it clear in the way I ought to speak" (Col 4:2–4). See also Colossians 4:11–13; James 5:16.

- *Doing any needed work in support of the preaching of the gospel.* "But I thought it necessary to send to you Epaphroditus, my brother and fellow worker and fellow soldier, who is also your messenger and minister to my need" (Phil 2:25). See also Philippians 1:5; 2:19–30.

- *Showing hospitality and love.* "Not lagging behind in diligence, fervent in spirit, serving the Lord; rejoicing in hope, persevering in tribulation, devoted to prayer, contributing to the needs of the saints, practicing hospitality ... Rejoice with those who rejoice, and weep with those who weep" (Rom 12:11–13, 15). See also Hebrews 13:1–3.

- *Working to restore those who have fallen away.* "Brethren, even if a man is caught in any trespass, you who are spiritual, restore such a one in a spirit of gentleness; each one looking to yourself, lest you too be tempted. Bear one another's burdens, and thus fulfill the law of Christ" (Gal 6:1–2). See also James 5:19–20.

- *Teaching the gospel to others.* "And He said to them, "Go into all the world and preach the gospel to all creation. He who has believed and has been baptized shall be saved; but he who has disbelieved shall be condemned" (Mark 16:15–16). See also Matthew 28:18–20.

- *Recognizing and addressing the needs of fellow Christians.* "And we urge you, brethren, admonish the unruly, encourage the fainthearted, help the weak, be patient with all men" (1 Thess 5:14). See also Romans 15:1–3.

- *Giving cheerfully, generously, and unselfishly.* "Let each one do just as he has purposed in his heart; not grudgingly or under compulsion; for God

loves a cheerful giver" (2 Cor 9:7). See also Acts
4:32–37; 2 Corinthians 8–9.

In practical terms, what actions fall under some of the categories listed above? Singing from your heart. Helping serve
the Lord's Supper. Preparing the Lord's Supper. Helping in
the nursery. Helping teach a class. Inviting a friend to worship. Writing a missionary. Contributing specifically to good
works that please God. Complimenting a teacher. Thanking
an elder. Including those who are different in your group of
friends. Visiting the nursing home. Setting up chairs for the
youth devotional.

You get the picture. "The work of ministry" really does
include any good action which we do to the glory of God. And
we have God's word that He will not forget such actions (1
Cor 15:58; Col 3:22–24; Heb 6:10).

We find an excellent analogy in sports. Each athlete offers
a unique contribution to the success and victory of the team.
The primary issue is not one of personal fame or glory; players
ideally do not bicker over who plays each post. With mutual
submission to their coach, and a shared commitment to win-
ning, they work in harmony. Paul used this metaphor when
he wrote, "Only conduct yourselves in a manner worthy of the
gospel of Christ; so that whether I come and see you or remain
absent, I may hear of you that you are standing firm in one
spirit, with one mind striving together for the faith of the
gospel" (Phil 1:27). The words "striving together" translate
the Greek term *synathleo*, from which we derive our word,

"athlete." The prefix "syn" means "with" or "together," as in our word "synthesis."

The hymn "There is a Balm in Gilead" highlights this matter of unity and diversity, noting that we do not all serve in the same way. It says, "If you cannot sing like angels, if you cannot preach like Paul, you can tell the love of Jesus, and say He died for all." No one can do everything. Everyone can do something. When each of us does what God has enabled us to do, and what our leaders have equipped us to do, all that is needed will be done.

DISCUSSION QUESTIONS

1. Why might some people have too narrow a view of "the work of ministry"?

2. What are the dangers of thinking about Christians in terms of "clergy" (official or ordained ministers) and "laity" (ordinary Christians)?

3. Is it accurate to say, "Every Christian is a minister"? How so?

4. Suppose someone said, "It's dangerous to encourage every Christian to think of himself or herself as a minister." Do you agree or disagree? Why?

5. Suppose someone said, "You shouldn't describe cleaning the church building, operating the sound system, or raking

leaves for an elderly widow as ministry. Ministry is more special than that." Do you agree or disagree? Why?

6. Three outstanding ministers are described in Philippians 2:19–30 and Colossians 4:11–13. What impresses you most about these servants of God?

7. What would result if every Christian accepted and pursued a specific area of service in the local church?

8. How might such an attitude and atmosphere be developed?

SIX

ENCOURAGEMENT

Equipping implies encouraging, which Ephesians 4:11–16 clearly emphasizes. Equipping involves inspiring, motivating, and exhorting each servant of God in particular areas of service. Every Christian needs encouragement; every Christian can give encouragement. It has been well said that the church should be the most encouraging body on earth. Surely this mutual support, so vital to all of us, is part of the reason that the Lord established the church. Romans 12:9–21 discusses in detail some of the ways in which God meets our need for encouragement through the fellow members of His body.

The more we study God's word, the more we'll be impressed by its balance. Some seem to think that encouragement means "no negatives." They seem to see encouragers as people who always notice and mention only the positive. Jesus didn't take that view (Matt 23). Neither did Paul, as can be seen in verse 14 of our text. Christian encouragers don't deny reality. They don't pretend that things are better than they are. Christian encouragers know that Jesus is the answer to our every need and that God is greater than anything. So, for example, we encourage each other to repent of sin and seek God's forgiveness. That's not negative; it's biblical!

THE POWER OF ENCOURAGEMENT

According to Ephesians 4:12–13, encouragement moves believers toward "the unity of the faith and of the knowledge of the Son of Man." Encouragement contributes to maturity and Christ-likeness. Encouragement helps each Christian do his or her share and causes growth of the body. And if we understand verse 16 correctly, that growth leads to even more encouragement. Seen in that light, anything that helps us imitate Jesus Christ is encouraging, even if it may seem difficult, painful, or challenging.

What makes encouragement so powerful? The encouragement we're discussing is grounded in God's love and God's truth. It flows from God's gift of Jesus Christ and Christ's gift of salvation. It's a natural result of God's forgiveness and our hope in Christ. It's the kind of encouragement we read about in Acts 11:23. The apostles sent Barnabas to Antioch because they had heard great things about the church there. Acts 4:32–37 and 11:24 may tell us why Barnabas was the man they sent. Verse 23 reads, "When he came and had seen the grace of God, he was glad, and encouraged them all that with purpose of heart they should continue with the Lord." Notice also verse 24: "for he was a good man, and full of the Holy

Spirit and of faith. And considerable numbers were brought
to the Lord" (Acts 11:24).

Barnabas is a model encourager. He started early. Scripture notes: "And Joseph, a Levite of Cyprian birth, who was
also called Barnabas by the apostles (which translated means
Son of Encouragement), and who owned a tract of land, sold
it and brought the money and laid it at the apostles' feet"
(Acts 4:36–37). "Son of" suggests "characterized by;" we
might call him, in our vernacular, "Mr. Encouragement." Before we read of even one encouraging word which he spoke,
we learn of his powerful example. Actions speak louder than
words, and this wonderful man uplifted many by his sacrificial
gift.

He encouraged even when risk was involved. Acts 9:26–
28 states: "And when he had come to Jerusalem, he was
trying to associate with the disciples; and they were all afraid
of him, not believing that he was a disciple. But Barnabas took
hold of him and brought him to the apostles and described to
them how he had seen the Lord on the road, and that He had
talked to him, and how at Damascus he had spoken out boldly
in the name of Jesus. And he was with them moving about
freely in Jerusalem, speaking out boldly in the name of the
Lord." Once Barnabas vouched for Saul, the church accepted
him. How highly that speaks of Barnabas' character and
influence!

He made sure that the work in Antioch was truly God's
work before he encouraged those brethren (Acts 11:23). Barnabas encouraged people near and far. He traveled to Antioch
to encourage. He left Antioch to seek Saul and involve him in

the work. "And when he had found him, he brought him to Antioch. And it came about that for an entire year they met with the church, and taught considerable numbers; and the disciples were first called Christians in Antioch" (Acts 11:25–26).

Start with a good man, full of the Holy Spirit and faith. That man is sure to encourage others, both by word and deed, to become Christ-like as well. The inevitable result is the conversion of many and the growth of the church. It's no wonder that when the Holy Spirit called a mission team, He chose Barnabas and Saul (Acts 13:1–4).

"Barnabas and Saul" soon began to be called "Paul and Barnabas" (Acts 13:42–43, for example). Paul, rather than Barnabas, was considered to be the chief speaker (Acts 14:12). It is remarkable that this great encourager gladly took the back seat as Paul became more prominent in their missionary efforts. A key component of encouragement is selflessness. Pride and self-promotion will stifle and kill encouragement any day.

Without Barnabas, would Saul have ever been welcomed by the church in Jerusalem? Without Barnabas, would Saul have ever become part of God's work in Antioch? Without their mutual encouragement, would Barnabas and Saul have become such an effective mission team? Without Barnabas, would John Mark have just "quit" (Acts 15:36–41)? We know that the Lord would have found a way for His will to be done. We also know that He used the Son of Encouragement in a powerful way.

God also encouraged Paul through Titus, who brought him encouraging news from Corinth. The apostle wrote: "For indeed, when we came to Macedonia, our bodies had no rest, but we were troubled on every side. Outside were conflicts, inside were fears. Nevertheless God, who comforts the downcast, comforted us by the coming of Titus, and not only by his coming, but also by the consolation with which he was comforted in you, when he told us of your earnest desire, your mourning, your zeal for me, so that I rejoiced even more" (2 Cor 7:5–7). Since Paul was at times troubled, afraid, and downcast, we can expect ourselves and others to be, also. As Titus blessed Paul, we can bless others, even church leaders who seem to be so strong.

HOW CAN WE BECOME BETTER ENCOURAGERS?

How can we become better equipped for the ministry of encouragement? We have offered three answers already.

- We can notice and appreciate how much emphasis Scripture gives to the power of encouragement in the growth of the church.
- We can remind ourselves of the opposition that we face.
- We can learn from and be motivated by the examples of powerful encouragers like Barnabas and Titus.

What else can we do to excel in the ministry of encouragement? We can train ourselves to notice when others do good. Most of us have high expectations. If we're not careful, we tend to expect the good and to notice only when things go wrong. That approach is dangerous and discouraging. It's not that we refuse to face problems; rather it's that we understand the power of a good word. We consistently look for opportunities to say something encouraging.

We can train ourselves to speak encouragingly when we do have opportunity. If we're not careful, we tend to intend to be encouraging. That is, we never get around to saying the good word, sending the nice note, or making the encouraging call. In this case, it's action, not intention that counts (Matt 21:28–32; Jam 2:14–17).

Finally, we can choose to be around encouraging people and to learn from them. Just as "evil company corrupts good habits," good company helps us build good habits (1 Cor 11:1 and 15:33).

Imagine that your phone rings first thing tomorrow morning, just as your day begins. The caller says, "I just want to tell you how grateful I am for your friendship, your faith, and your service to Christ. You are a blessing in my life. Keep up the good work and know that I am praying for you." What difference would that make in your attitude, your activities, and your effectiveness?

Now anticipate, not *receiving* such a call that makes your day, but *placing* that call to someone else. You will inspire the same joy and confidence in others that you would gain if they contacted you. Pick several this week, from the prayer list, the sick list, or the visitor list. Surprise them with a "thinking of you" card, a visit, or a phone call. Instead of asking, "Why hasn't anyone encouraged me?" try asking, "Whom can I encourage?" No matter your circumstances, there are others whose load you can lift.

We are the vessels through which God's comfort and consolation will flow to others (2 Cor 1:3–11). God will uplift, love, and bless those around us by means of our words and actions. Encouragers receive more than they give. As a result of encouraging others, we will become more gracious, godly, and caring people than ever before. There is no greater source of joy and fulfillment to be found.

In the church, all of us are to be active in mutual encouragement. "But encourage one another day after day, as long as it is still called 'Today,' lest anyone of you be hardened by the deceitfulness of sin" (Heb 3:13). Encouragement is one vital purpose for our assembly. "Not forsaking our own assembling together, as is the habit of some, but encouraging one another; and all the more, as you see the day drawing near" (Heb 10:25).

Not only does it work in both directions, it spreads to other people, too. When another person encourages us, we want to pass it on to the next person we see. We give and receive. We lift and are lifted. We love and are loved. And in all of it we see God at work.

DISCUSSION QUESTIONS

1. Is encouragement really as powerful as is claimed in this lesson? Offer examples from Scripture and from your own life.

2. Do Christians need encouragement from one another? After all, we have God's word.

3. Think of the most encouraging Christian whom you know. What can you learn from that person? How can he or she help us to excel in encouragement?

4. Some seem to believe, "Encouragers are born, not made. Either a person has the knack, or he doesn't." Do you agree or disagree? Give reasons for your answer.

5. Some people are not naturally expressive or outgoing. In what specific ways could such individuals, in keeping with their personality, still offer encouragement?

6. Do you think Jesus as a man needed encouragement? If so, when?

7. Would you agree that more people quit serving God for lack of encouragement than for any other reason? If so, why?

8. Is one justified in quitting—ceasing to be involved in ministry—if words of encouragement do not come when needed? Explain.

SEVEN
BUILDING UNITY

The unity of believers has always been important to God and essential to His cause. Psalm 133 begins, "Behold how good and how pleasant it is for brethren to dwell together in unity." After a time of civil strife following the death of King Saul, the Israelites to the north joined the people of Judah in acknowledging David as their ruler (2 Sam 5:1–5). The result was a period of unprecedented peace and victory, which would have been impossible without such harmony. Amos asked the rhetorical question, "Can two walk together, unless they are agreed?" (Amos 3:3) The obvious answer is, "No."

Just before His betrayal and crucifixion, Jesus prayed specifically for the unity of all believers (John 17:20–26). He said in part, "I do not ask in behalf of these alone, but for those also who believe in Me through their word; that they may all be one; even as Thou, Father, art in Me, and I in Thee, that they also may be in Us; that the world may believe that Thou didst send Me" (John 17:20–21). With so much at stake, namely the faith of the world, unity is seen to have inestimable value.

Paul identifies "endeavoring to keep the unity of the Spirit in the bond of peace" as a key aspect of Christians walking worthy of our calling (Eph 4:1–3). Ephesians 4:16 speaks of the unity of the whole body "joined and knit together."

THE BASIS FOR UNITY

Please review the concluding section of Lesson 1. Christian unity is based on the oneness of God Himself. Monotheism, the doctrine that God is one, is the foundation of all His commandments, both in the Old Testament (Deut 6:4) and the New (Mark 12:28–33). It is just because there is one God that there is one faith, one baptism, one body, and one hope. It is because God is one that we are to be one. This is seen in a special way in marriage, in which God takes two and makes them one flesh (Gen 2:18–25). Therefore, man is not to separate or put asunder husband and wife, because the Lord has united them (Matt 19:3–6).

Furthermore, unity is based on the oneness of truth. Our unity flows from our love for God and our loyalty to Him. Scripture always speaks of truth in the singular, never the plural. Hear what Jesus said: "You shall know the truth, and the truth shall make you free" (John 8:32). "I am the way, and the truth, and the life; no one comes to the Father, but through Me" (John 14:6). "Sanctify them in the truth; Thy word is truth" (John 17:17). "For this I have been born, and for this I have come into the world, to bear witness to the truth. Everyone who is of the truth hears My voice" (John 18:37).

The center and source of unity is Christ Himself. Ephesians 2:11–22 praises Jesus Christ as the cornerstone of Christian unity, even between formerly estranged Gentiles and Jews. That passage says in part, "But now in Christ Jesus you who formerly were far off have been brought near by the blood of Christ. For He Himself is our peace, who made both groups into one, and broke down the barrier of the dividing wall, by abolishing in His flesh the enmity, which is the Law of commandments contained in ordinances, that in Himself He might make the two into one new man, thus establishing peace, and might reconcile them both in one body to God through the cross, by it having put to death the enmity" (Eph 2:13–16).

On that cornerstone is laid the foundation of the apostles and prophets. As God's inspired spokesmen, they wrote and revealed God's guiding truth. All who stand on that unchanging, immovable rock must stand together in harmony. We must invite the people of the world to plant themselves beside us on that same rock. It is the cross that tears down the barriers between us. Lest we miss how personally God regards the unity of believers, let us notice that verse 14 begins, "For He [Jesus Christ] Himself is our peace." Jesus explained the unifying power of the cross when He said, "And I, if I be lifted up from the earth, will draw all men to Myself" (John 12:32). The closer we draw to His sacrificial death, the closer we will find ourselves to each other.

The Lord knows that we live in a fragmented world. This world is divided by gender, race, and ethnicity. It's divided by politics, preferences, and perspectives. It's divided by competing doctrines, competing religions, and even competing gods. All that being true, the unity of believers is going to take work. Like any good thing, it doesn't just happen. Satan has used a "divide-and-conquer" strategy to weaken and demoralize the church, and he has had plenty of human help to carry out that strategy.

Jesus used brilliant logic regarding unity and division to prove His claim to be the Christ, sent from the Father and full of His Spirit. When He cast out demons, His critics were unable to refute such miracles. So they attributed Jesus' power to Beelzebub, the prince of demons, Satan. Jesus responded, "And if a kingdom is divided against itself, that kingdom cannot stand. And if a house is divided against itself, that house will not be able to stand. And if Satan has risen up against himself and is divided, he cannot stand, but he is finished!" (Mark 3:24–26) When the United States faced civil war, President Lincoln presented his famous "House Divided" speech, based on Jesus' teaching.

Though the Lord Himself is the source of true unity, He blesses us by allowing us to share in the process of building unity. We say "true unity" because there are counterfeit versions. Ephesians 4:13 speaks of "the unity of the faith and of the knowledge of the Son of God." This is the unity we work to build.

BUILDING UNITY

Nothing builds unity like working together for a common cause. In the immediate aftermath of the events of September 11, 2001, our nation was reminded of that truth in a powerful way. Paul clearly stresses that truth in Ephesians 4:11–16.

God gave some to be spiritual leaders "for the equipping of the saints for the work of ministry, for the edifying of the body of Christ, till we all come to the unity of the faith and of the knowledge of the Son of God." There are no accidents in Scripture. When God's people become equipped for the work of ministry, they encourage one another, and the unity of the body is enhanced. Working together for a common cause has always enhanced unity.

On a negative note, read Genesis 11:1–10. The people did not want to scatter over the earth. They decided to oppose God's will by building a tower as a symbol of their unity. "And the Lord said, 'Indeed the people are one and they all have one language, and this is what they begin to do; now nothing that they propose to do will be withheld from them'" (Gen 11:6). To stop their plan, the Lord had to break their unity. Even those who oppose God are powerful when they are united.

On a positive note, remember Ezra and Nehemiah. A hopeless group of Jews had returned to Jerusalem. Their enemies had so discouraged them that all work on the city wall had stopped. Faithful Nehemiah found himself facing a terrible situation. But Nehemiah succeeded in uniting the people. After years of failure and despite strong opposition, the wall was soon joined together up to half its height (Neh 4:6). Nehemiah's famous explanation is, "For the people had a mind to work." He united them behind a common cause.

There is no greater cause than the cause of Christ. There is no greater ministry than the Lord's ministry of reconciling men to God (Rom 5:1–11; 2 Cor 5:12–21). There is no greater knowledge than the knowledge of the Son of God (Phil 3:7–16).

It is no wonder then that the Lord rebukes so strongly those who would divide what He has united. "Reject a factious man after a first and second warning, knowing that such a man is perverted and is sinning, being self-condemned" (Titus 3:10–11). "Now I urge you, brethren, keep your eye on those who cause dissensions and hindrances contrary to the teaching which you learned, and turn away from them. For such men are slaves, not of our Lord Christ but of their own appetites; and by their smooth and flattering speech they deceive the hearts of the unsuspecting" (Rom 16:17–18).

Ephesians 4:17–24 explains that, because of Christ, everything about us has changed. We have a new walk, a new mindset, and a new direction. We are directed to "lay aside the old self, which is being corrupted in accordance with the lusts of deceit," and to "be renewed in the spirit of your mind, and put on the new self, which in the likeness of God has been created in righteousness and holiness of the truth" (Eph 4:22–24). It is plain to see that two people, or a million people, who share the new nature of Christ, according to His Word, will think, serve and work together in true unity.

This unity is much more than a mere theory. Paul offers a wonderful set of practical instructions for building unity in Ephesians 4:25–32. These instructions equip Christians to work powerfully for the unity of the body.

- Cease all lying and speak the truth with one another (v. 25). Deceit and falsehoods divide; honesty and transparency unite.
- Control your anger lest it lead you to sin (v. 26–27). Hatred destroys the container that holds it; malice makes intimacy impossible.
- Steal nothing: rather work so that you can share with those in need (v. 28). Instead of "helping yourself" to the things of others, help others with the things that are yours.
- Control your tongue (v. 29). Use your speech to encourage. Sticks and stones may break bones, but rotten, corrupt words break hearts. Speech that serves and strengthens will form strong spiritual bonds.
- Guard your heart (v. 31). Don't let sin take up residence there. What your heart desires, your mouth, hands, and feet will express and pursue.
- Forgive one another, just like God has forgiven you in Christ (v. 32). People who are both forgiven and forgiving are bound inseparably in spirit.

DISCUSSION QUESTIONS

1. Is unity as precious and powerful as this lesson asserts? Explain.

2. Is unity as difficult to achieve and maintain as this lesson asserts? Explain.

3. Why was unity so important to Jesus?

4. This lesson offered two examples of working for a common cause building unity. What other examples can you add?

5. Why do some people prefer to be isolated rather than to unite with others?

6. Describe one or more ministries in your congregation which are working well because of the unity among the people involved.

7. How important is unity for the growth of the church?

8. Paul's instructions in Ephesians 4:25–32 seem so simple and clear. Why do Christians often find them difficult to follow?

EIGHT
LIKE JESUS

You know the old saying, "Practice makes perfect." More accurately, "Practice makes permanent," which may or may not be good. A recent revision offers an important correction: "Perfect practice makes perfect." If we're practicing wrong, then there's no magic in the number of repetitions. Repetition helps only if we have the right pattern.

The same is true of ministry. There is one perfect pattern. When we look to the example of Jesus Christ and to the truth of His word, we can become equipped for authentic, lasting, God-honoring ministry.

JESUS AND MINISTRY

The ministry of Jesus was characterized by complete devotion to God the Father. We see this first in Luke 2:49 when Jesus asked his earthly parents, "Why did you seek Me? Did you not know that I must be about My Father's business?" We see it again in John 4:34 as Jesus says to His disciples, "My food

is to do the will of Him who sent Me, and to finish His work."
It is fully stated in John 8:29, "And He who sent me is with
Me. The Father has not left Me alone, for I always do those
things that please Him." The Lord's devotion and faithfulness
to the Father are also vividly described in Philippians 2:5–11
and in Hebrews 5:5–8.

Jesus' perfect devotion to the Father allowed Him to say,
"If you had known Me, you would have known My Father
also...He who has seen Me has seen the Father." (John 14:7–
11). Of course John had already said of Him, "No one has
seen God at any time. The only begotten Son, who is in the
bosom of the Father, He has declared Him" (John 1:18). The
Lord's prayer of John 17 further emphasizes the Son's devotion to His Father, ending with the passionate words, "O
righteous Father! The world has not known You, but I have
known You; and these have known that You sent Me. And I
have declared to them Your name, and will declare it, that the
love with which You loved Me may be in them, and I in them"
(John 17:25–26).

The ministry of Jesus was characterized by selfless service. His first miracle was not at the time or the place of His
choosing. At His mother's urging, He "rescued" a wedding
from severe embarrassment (John 2:1–12). When His prayers were interrupted, He served by preaching and casting out
demons (Mark 1:35–39). When His sermon was interrupted
by four men lowering their friend through the roof, He noted
their faith and healed the man (Mark 2:1–5). When the mul-
titudes followed Him for the wrong motives, He loved them
and taught them (John 6:22–27). He urged them to believe

unto salvation (John 6:29, 40, 47). Even from the cross He reached out to meet the needs of His mother and of the penitent thief (John 19:25–27; Luke 23:42–43).

When Paul was teaching the Philippians to avoid selfish ambition and to look out for the interests of others, he appealed to the ultimate example of Christ (Phil 2:1–11). He reminded those brethren how Jesus "made Himself of no reputation, taking on the form of a bondservant and coming in the likeness of men." He reminded them and us how "He humbled Himself, and became obedient to the point of death, even the death of the cross." Indeed, no one took the life of Jesus for the sins of the world. He offered it freely (John 10:1–18).

The ministry of Jesus was characterized by great compassion. When John's disciples asked the famous question, "Are You the Coming One, or do we look for another" (Luke 7:19), Jesus gave them an answer that documented both the fulfillment of Scripture (Isa 61:1–3) and God's own compassion (Luke 7:22). We see the compassion of Christ as He cleansed the leper by touching him (Luke 5:12–16). We see His compassion as He forgave the sinful woman in the Pharisee's house (Luke 7:36–50). We are told that compassion led Him to feed the 5,000 (Mark 8:2). He showed compassion to tax collectors and sinners (Luke 15). When criticized for deeming such people worthy of His presence, He offered the classic response, "Those who are well have no need of a physician, but those who are sick. I did not come to call the righteous, but sinners, to repentance" (Mark 2:17). Jesus knew what they were, and He loved them anyway. Both the Father and the

Son knew what we were outside Christ, but They loved us anyway (Rom 5:6–11)!

Jesus even had compassion for the people who rejected Him and were about to take His life (Matt 23:37–39). How could there be any greater compassion than having the first gospel sermon preached to the very people who crucified Him (Acts 2)? When it comes to compassion, Jesus shows us the heart of hearts. Hebrews 4:14–16 beautifully documents His continuing ability to sympathize with us in our every weakness.

The ministry of Jesus was characterized by strong desire to meet people's greatest need: their need to be right with God. Jesus fed the 5,000, but he also taught them about God, offering them "the bread of life" (John 6:48–58). He forgave the woman who was taken in adultery, but He also told her, "Go and sin no more" (John 8:11–12). He didn't just offer water to the woman at the well; He offered her "living water" (John 4:1–42). Jesus was never content just to attract a crowd; He rejected that temptation, as recorded in Matthew 4:1–7. He always called those who heard Him to eternal life (John 6).

The ministry of Jesus was characterized by fervent prayer. Mark 1:35 tells us that Jesus arose "a long while before daylight" to pray in a solitary place. Luke 5:16 simply says, "So He Himself often withdrew into the wilderness and prayed." Luke 6:12 tells us what He did the night before choosing the twelve: "He went out to the mountain to pray, and continued all night in prayer to God."

Believers continue to be moved by the beauty and simplicity of His model prayer (Matt 6:8–15). We continue to be moved by the passion and depth of His prayers on the night of the betrayal (Matt 26:36–46). We believe that even the fact that His disciples asked Him to teach them to pray is evidence of what they saw Him doing so regularly (Luke 11:1–4). It may be far more than that. It may be that they saw evidence of the effectiveness of His prayers (Jam 5:16).

The ministry of Jesus was characterized by challenging, engaging teaching. He showed tremendous skill in helping questioners, even those with poor motives, assess their own understanding of Scripture (Luke 10:25–26). He agreed with people when they were correct in their understanding (Luke 10:28, 37; Mark 12:34). Still, He was willing to let people face the weight of their own inconsistencies and misunderstandings (Mark 11:27–33). He effectively employed logic in upholding the truth of Scripture (Mark 12:24–27). He reframed dangerous questions in ways that made them opportunities to learn (Matt 22:15–22). He used profound stories to engage people in thoughtful learning (Luke 10:25–37; Luke 15). And, He always faithfully upheld the word of God (Matthew 5:17–19; 24:35).

The ministry of Jesus was characterized by involving others in God's service. We see this in such "small matters" as using a boy's lunch to feed a multitude (John 6:1–14) and borrowing the colt on which He made the triumphal entry (Mark 11:1–6). We see it in accepting help from godly women who "provided for Him from their substance" (Luke 8:1–3) and in allowing a grateful woman to anoint His body for burial

(Mark 14:3–9). We see it in His allowing Andrew to bring Peter, Philip to bring Nathaniel, and a Samaritan woman to bring her entire village (John 1:35–46; 4:27–30). We see it in the sending of the twelve, the sending of the seventy, and the sending of every Christian for world evangelism (Luke 9 and 10; Matt 28:18–20).

The ministry of Jesus was characterized by abounding joy over faith and repentance. When a centurion stated his faith that Jesus could heal whether present or distant, "He marveled and said to those who followed, 'Assuredly, I say to you, I have not found such great faith, not even in Israel'" (Matt 8:10). He embraced all who did the will of the Father as His own brethren (Matt 12:46–50). As He removed the affliction of her daughter, He praised the humble Canaanite mother, "O woman, great is your faith! Let it be as you desire" (Matt 15:28). He included the feast of celebration in His parable of the prodigal son (Luke 15:11–32). Then, He showed that very joy as He witnessed the repentance of Zacchaeus (Luke 19:1–10).

IMITATING JESUS IN MINISTRY

It is true that we do not have the supernatural insight which Jesus had. We do not receive direct, private communication from God. We cannot claim to approach the level of wisdom and discernment shown by Jesus.

Nevertheless, we know that Jesus is our pattern in all things good. We know this as we understand the meaning of the word "disciple." A disciple is one who follows, imitates, and learns from. Matthew 10:24–25a state the matter clearly: "A disciple is not above his teacher, nor a servant above his master. It is enough for a disciple that he be like his teacher, and a servant like his master."

The earliest Christians embraced this truth and followed His example of involvement. They personally sacrificed to meet the needs of others (Acts 2:43–44; 4:32–37). They participated in choosing additional leaders (Acts 6:1–7). Prayer permeated their lives (Acts 1:24, 2:42, 4:23-31, & 6:3-4). When persecution arose, "Those who were scattered abroad went everywhere preaching the word" (Acts 8:4). Their example, along with the admonitions of Ephesians 4:11–16, stands as powerful encouragement to us. What they did, we can do, if we embrace their attitude and imitate their faith.

We can know that we are being rightly equipped for the work of ministry if we are learning to follow the example of Jesus. Following His example will certainly include:

- Devotion to God, seeking first the kingdom of God and His righteousness (Matt 6:33).
- Selfless service (Phil 2:1–4; Rom 12:9–21).
- Growing compassion, especially for the lost (Matt 9:35–38).
- A focus on spiritual needs, especially the need to be in Christ (Acts 2:40; Rom 9:1–5).
- Faithful teaching of God's truth in love (Eph 4:15).
- Continual, fervent prayer (Mark 1:35; Luke 5:16; Matt 26:36–46).

DISCUSSION QUESTIONS

1. If you had to choose one characteristic of Jesus' ministry as the most important example for Christians today, which would you choose? Why?

2. If you had to choose one characteristic of Jesus' ministry as the most challenging for Christians today, which would you choose? Why?

3. If you had to choose one characteristic of Jesus' ministry as the most misunderstood by Christians today, which would you choose? Why?

4. We know that Jesus is our ultimate example. In the area of ministry, why might some be tempted to follow other examples?

5. How do statements like those of 1 Corinthians 11:1 and Philippians 3:17 help us as we seek to follow Christ's example?

6. What can we do to help ourselves follow the example of Jesus more fully? What specific steps can we take?

7. What specific steps can we take to help our brethren more fully follow the example of Jesus?

NINE
HOW IS IT DONE?

Have you noticed that Paul, at least in our text, never tells church leaders specifically how to equip the saints for the work of ministry? Have you ever wondered why he doesn't? Part of the answer may be God's foreknowledge that Christian ministry would extend over many centuries in tremendously diverse cultures. Part of the answer may be that God gives us exactly what we need and expects us to grow through the process of implementing His commands. One answer is clear: giving "how to" instructions was not Paul's purpose in this passage. His emphasis here is on the purpose and results of the equipping. While we acknowledge that, we still see the need to ask, "How can spiritual leaders accomplish the important job of equipping the saints for the work of ministry?"

Perhaps the most natural first answer is by teaching. After all, that's what this series of lessons is attempting to do. Lesson 1 discussed the importance of a teachable spirit. Lesson 2 began by saying, "Christianity is a taught religion." But, what do we mean by "teaching"?

In the context of the local church, teaching may first bring to mind the sermon and the Bible class. While these are biblical and effective means of teaching, they certainly aren't the only ones.

Many Bible school programs, particularly at the teen and adult level, follow what we might describe as the standard school approach: the teacher talks, and the students listen. While we know that thorough knowledge of God's word is vital, this style of teaching may not be the best way to accomplish the equipping of God's people for the work of ministry. Perhaps you have heard the adage, "Tell me, and I'll forget. Show me, and I'll remember. Involve me, and I'll learn." Even allowing for a bit of overstatement, there's truth in that adage.

While some training has to precede doing, some things can be learned only by doing them. No matter how thoroughly you might read a repair manual for your car, the test comes when you raise the hood and start with the wrenches. One can read every book ever written about how to ride a bicycle, but the practical side of knowledge comes only through experience. Attending lectures about running a marathon can't make a person a marathon runner. The same is true of ministry. So much of it is fully learned only as it is lived.

EXPANDING OUR THINKING

Wise leaders would never limit the concept of teaching to the worship and Bible class hours. Wise leaders remember God's instructions to parents and grandparents in Deuteronomy 6:1–9. Verse 4 gives the foundation for sound teaching; it flows from faith in God. Within the home and the church, teachers begin by getting their own hearts and actions right (v. 5). Until we genuinely love the Lord and translate that love into godly behavior, we are not qualified to teach (v. 6). To be credible and effective, teachers must show respect for God and His truth. They must know the Word and model obedience to God's commands.

Wise teachers teach continually. That's the heart of Deuteronomy 6:7–9. Some emphasize the importance of seizing "teachable moments" as such moments are encountered in the ebb and flow of daily life. Regrettably, these opportunities are not always apparent. The best way to seize such moments is to teach continually. We see Jesus embracing this principle as He chose the twelve. The wording of Mark 3:14 is impressive: "Then He appointed twelve, that they might be with Him and that He might send them out to teach." There was something vital about being with Jesus. There was also something obvious about being with Jesus. The Sanhedrin could not credit the boldness of Peter and John to formal education or training. Rather, "...They realized that they had been with Jesus" (Acts 4:13). They had the attitude, the manner, the confidence, and the faith of Christ. And they learned these from the Master Himself.

There is another crucial reason that godly leaders choose to teach continually. Learners, whether children or adults, don't come with an off switch. Sometimes it seems that they pay even more attention to the things that we whisper. In the spirit of Deuteronomy 6, even our whispers should be diligently aimed at promoting faith in God. Even our whispers should be echoes of His word. On top of that, people generally see better than they hear. In addition to our words, our tone, our attitude, and our actions teach. Someone is always watching. Someone is always learning. That should make us even more conscious of the 24/7/365 nature of our teaching.

No, we cannot physically walk with Jesus today. However, we can "walk in the light as He is in the light" (1 John 1:7). We can and "should follow in His steps." (1 Peter 2:21). As we serve God together, we should all aspire to the dual roles of follower and leader in the spirit of 1 Corinthians 11:1, 16:15–16, and Philippians 3:15. For better or worse, everybody is somebody's leader. We make the choice to lead wisely.

Wise teachers would never limit themselves to one means of teaching God's truth. They know that some people learn primarily by listening. Others learn best when they can see what is being taught. Some don't learn much unless the process is "hands on." Could this be why Jesus taught in sermons, in parables, through His silence, and through His actions (Matt 5–7, 13; John 8:6; Luke 5:12–13)? Could this be why Jesus asked His disciples questions and involved them in His work (John 6:1–14; Matt 10)? Could this be one reason Paul involved so many fellow workers in his mission efforts?

Wise teachers use every available means to teach God's truth. God has always used a multi-media approach to teaching. He had Ezekiel use signs, symbols, and shocking object lessons (Ezek 4–5, 17:1–10, and 24:1–14.) He helped Paul use an idolatrous altar as a visual aid and quote from Greek poets as he preached the gospel in Athens (Acts 17). He affirmed an accurate and unflattering description of the Cretans by moving Paul to quote one of their own prophets (Titus 1:12). As with Peter and John in Acts 4, even Paul's legal defense became an opportunity to tell of his conversion and his commission as apostle to the Gentiles (Acts 27). Jesus used current events to drive home crucial points (Luke 13:1–5).

Wise teachers know the importance of modeling both attitudes and skills. Paul reminded Timothy to "instruct the brethren," to "command and teach," and to "be an example to the brethren" (1 Tim 4:6–16). In the second letter he added, "And the things that you have heard from me among many witnesses, commit these to faithful men who will be able to teach others also" (2 Tim 2:2). Clearly, the process of equipping was to be ongoing. Those who become equipped become equippers. The cycle of mentoring never ends.

WILLING LEARNERS

Both Ephesians 4:11–16 and Proverbs 6:1–9 assume a fundamental willingness to learn. Both assume a positive orientation toward growth, a desire to become godlier. Regrettably, not every Christian shares that orientation.

We live in an age of "plausible deniability." Some reason, "The less I know the better. The less I know, the less I have to do. The less I know, the less the Lord can hold me accountable for." How sad! How errant! How ungrateful!

This attitude is the ultimate burial of one's talent (Matt 25:14–30). It is a clear rejection of every biblical mandate for faithfulness and spiritual growth (Matt 7:21–27; 2 Pet 1:5–11). It is a clear rejection of every biblical mandate for serving and loving our brethren (Rom 12:3–21; Phil 2:3–4; 1 Pet 4:7–11). This attitude puts one's soul in jeopardy (Heb 5:12–6:6).

So, how can spiritual leaders most effectively work to equip the saints for the work of ministry? Certainly, teaching by precept is needed. At the same time, what if we ask, "What is the most effective means of teaching hospital visitation? Evangelistic door knocking? How to conduct a home Bible study? How to encourage a struggling brother?" There is no substitute for "hands on" experience. Growing congregations provide maximum opportunity for such experience. In doing so, they follow the mandate of Ephesians 4:11–16.

Regrettably, there may be congregations that fail to provide sufficient opportunity for equipping. If so, how can a growing Christian best seek such "hands on" training? Consider the following suggestions:

- Ask an elder or a minister if you can make visits with him one evening each week.
- Ask an effective, evangelistic friend to take you along on the next Bible study.

- Identify any effective ministry within the congregation. Ask one of its leaders how you can help. As you help, watch, ask questions, and learn.
- Identify a need and, with the elders' guidance, begin a ministry to meet that need.
- Take a personal evangelism or practical ministry class. If you can't take the class in person, take it online.
- Begin an evangelistic Bible study in your home.
- Ask God to send opportunities for service. Not only will He do so, asking Him for that blessing will open our eyes to opportunities that are already present.
- Gladly accept any opportunity to serve. God gives increased ability and opportunity to those who are faithful (Matt 25:21, 23, 29).

We repeat a key point: some things can be learned only by doing them. Christian ministry is serving others to the glory of God. Faithful ministry is walking in the very steps of Jesus (Matt 20:28). While God's word can teach us so much about ministry, mature understanding comes only as we practice God's truth.

DISCUSSION QUESTIONS

1. In your experience, how effective has your congregation been in equipping the saints for the work of ministry?

2. What obstacles have worked to hinder effective equipping? Name some efforts which have been particularly effective.

3. How might the effectiveness of Bible classes in equipping the saints be improved?

4. What does Proverbs 22:6 help us understand about the process of equipping?

5. Are Paul's instructions to Timothy in 1 Timothy 4:6–16 and 2 Timothy 2:2 applicable today? Explain.

6. Who is more responsible for equipping the saints for the work of ministry, church leaders or the saints themselves? Explain.

7. How can we become more willing learners?

8. Do you agree with the final statement made in this lesson, "Mature understanding comes only as we practice God's truth"? Explain.

TEN
THE MATURITY FACTOR

Ministry helps us mature. Our text says this repeatedly. As Christians are equipped for ministry and the church is encouraged:

- We grow in the unity of the faith.
- We grow toward the measure of the stature of the fullness of Christ.
- We become more secure and stable in the faith.
- We grow up in all things into Him who is the head—Christ.

THE NEED FOR MATURITY

Scripture sometimes speaks of immature Christians as "babes in Christ" (1 Cor 3:1; Heb 5:13). Paul does much the same in our text when he speaks of "children, tossed to and fro and carried about with every wind of doctrine" (Eph 4:14). Just as with our physical development, spiritual childhood is a necessary stage. While it has its challenges and its beauty, it is neither natural nor desirable to remain at that stage. God expects His children to grow up (Heb 5:12–6:3; 1 Pet 2:1–3; 2 Pet 1:1–11).

Spiritual immaturity presents numerous dangers. The immature are gullible. They often pursue "foolish and ignorant disputes," failing to realize that such only "generate strife" (2 Tim 2:23). They lack the ability to discern the "weightier matters of the law" and to give such matters proper emphasis without neglecting even the smallest obedience (Matt 23:23). Some find it easy to be judgmental toward those who have different convictions, even when such differences do not violate God's truth (Rom 14:1–13). Others are easily influenced to violate their own consciences (Rom 14:14–23).

The spiritually immature find it easy to scratch their "itching ears" by turning "away from the truth" and turning aside to fables (2 Tim 4:3–4). They forget the power of the adversary, that "we wrestle not against flesh and blood, but against principalities, against powers, against the rulers of the darkness of this age, against spiritual hosts of wickedness in the heavenly places" (Eph 6:12; 1 Tim 4:1–5). They forget that those who do not love and believe the truth will be abandoned by God (2 Thess 2:9–12).

Such people may speak religious language, think religious thoughts, and do religious acts, but they lack spiritual security in Christ. Scripture speaks of them in fearful terms. They are those "having a form of godliness, but denying its power" (2 Tim 3:5). They are "always learning and never able to come to the knowledge of the truth" (2 Tim 3:7).

The immature are easy marks for Satan. Think of the "lion language" of 1 Peter 5:8–9. Remember those nature films that show a group of lions stalking a herd of prey? The young and the weak are the most frequent victims. Though Satan's attack is often more subtle, it is no less deadly.

Ephesians 4:14 reminds us that many competing messages oppose the truth of God. Some of those messages and some of those messengers are tricky, cunning, crafty, and deceitful. They don't wear signs that say, "Get your false message here!" In their most deadly form, they maintain the language and appearances of faithfulness. To the uninformed, their message looks remarkably like truth. Remember the example of the false prophet Hananiah? He seemed to be optimistic and patriotic, while many believed Jeremiah to be a faithless traitor (Jer 27). Only the spiritually mature would have discerned the truth. Remember the frightening truth of 2 Corinthians 11:14–15, "For Satan himself transforms himself into an angel of light. Therefore it is no great thing if his ministers also transform themselves into ministers of righteousness."

Nowhere is this danger more evident than in the book of Jude. Jude 4 speaks of false teachers as "certain men who have crept in unnoticed." While they attended the "love feasts," their goals were not loving (Jude 12). Jude 16–18 employs a litany of negatives in describing these ungodly purveyors of a false gospel.

THE TEST OF TRUTH

The test of truth comes in the real world. It comes as we face the trials of ministry. Untried faith is, by definition, weak. As the Hebrew writer reminds us, "Solid food belongs to those who are of full age, that is, those who by reason of use have their senses exercised to discern both good and evil" (Heb 5:14). "Use" and "exercise" are action words. They call us to ministry.

Christianity is a "real world religion." God's truth always passes the real-world test. But only those who have been equipped for ministry are prepared to take God's truth to the world. Our text emphasizes at least three aspects of this preparation.

First, there is the unity of the faith. As noted in Lesson 2, Scripture alone provides the doctrinal foundation for biblical unity. We still sometimes hear the phrase "grounded in the truth." It's a good phrase. It does not, as some assert, speak of being stagnant and limited. Rather, it speaks of stability, reliability, and steadiness. It speaks of absolute confidence in the inerrant, infallible word of God.

We remember Pilate's famous question, "What is truth?" (John 18:38). Both practically and philosophically, Pilate has many modern relatives. Scripture, however, is certain about truth. Jesus is and brings truth (John 14:6; 1:17). Jesus linked truth and salvation (John 8:31–32; 17:17). In biblical terms, truth is something that can be known, taught, obeyed, and practiced (John 8:32; Matt 22:16; Rom 2:8; Gal 3:1; 5:7; John 3:21).

Then, there is the knowledge of the Son of God. The best short definition of Christian maturity is simply Christ-likeness. As noted in Lesson 8, Jesus is our perfect pattern. Our greatest goal is to be like Him. Those who are like Jesus are anything but unstable. Those who are like Jesus believe and teach all the truth of God and only the truth of God (Acts 20:27; 1 Pet 4:11; Rev 22:18–21).

In keeping with Lesson 9, those who truly know Jesus know His heart and His ministry. Their knowledge is not merely academic or intellectual. They know something of "the power of His resurrection" because God has used that same power to raise them from the grave of baptism (Phil 3:10; Col 2:11–12). They know something of "the fellowship of His suffering, being conformed to His death" (Phil 3:10).

Finally, there is the recognition that there are competing doctrines and those who promote them. A crucial aspect of being equipped for the work of ministry is gaining the ability to recognize and resist those doctrines, without forsaking the spirit of Christ. The attitude with which we teach the truth and oppose error will be the focus of Chapter 11.

Are there biblical examples of believers who were "children tossed to and fro and carried about with every wind of doctrine"? The brethren in Galatia qualify. They were in danger of turning away from the grace of Christ to a different gospel (Gal 1:6–10). They were in danger of letting their actions say that "Christ died in vain" (Gal 3:21). They were in danger of falling from grace (Gal 5:4).

Some in Corinth qualify. They were following men rather than Christ (1 Cor 1:10–17). They were condoning immorality (1 Cor 5). They were litigating fellow brethren (1 Cor 6). They were perverting the Lord's Supper (1 Cor 11). They were even misusing miraculous spiritual gifts (1 Cor 12–14). On top of all, some were surrendering faith in the resurrected Christ (1 Cor 15).

Those in Colossae were warned, "Beware lest anyone cheat you through philosophy and empty deceit, according to the tradition of men, according to the basic principles of the world, and not according to Christ" (Col 2:8). Some of them thought that they could add to God's design for worship and holy living (Col 2:16–23). Somehow, they forgot the supremacy and the sufficiency of Christ (Col 2:9–10). That is one lesson which the mature in Christ never forget.

SPIRITUAL MATURITY

The mature are grounded, "established in the present truth" (2 Pet 1:12). They stand in the truth (John 8:44—If the devil "does not stand in the truth," surely God's people do.), in the gospel (1 Cor 15:1), and in grace (Rom 5:2). They are able to "stand against the wiles of the devil" because they have "put on the whole armor of God" (Eph 6:10–20). They stand, united and serving with brethren of like precious faith (Phil 1:27). They heed Paul's challenge, "Therefore, brethren, stand fast and hold the traditions which you were taught, whether by word or our epistle" (2 Thess 2:15).

The mature "count all things loss for the excellence of the knowledge of Christ Jesus" (Phil 3:8). They seek "the righteousness which is from God by faith" (Phil 3:9). They live as if the resurrection and judgment are certain. They do not count themselves to "have already attained;" rather they "press toward the goal for the prize of the upward call of God in Christ Jesus" (Phil 3:12–14). The mature choose to have their thinking and their actions guided by Scripture (Phil 3:15). The mature practice love as described in John 13:34–35, Romans 5:6–8, and 1 Corinthians 13.

The mature recognize that "The way of man is not in himself. It is not in man who walks to direct his own steps" (Jer 10:23–24; Prov 21:2). They relish the truth that "The fear of the Lord is the beginning of knowledge" and "the fear of the Lord is the beginning of wisdom." (Prov 1:7 and 9:10). The mature recognize the importance of choosing friends wisely (Psa 101; Prov 13:20; 22:24–25). They realize that while proper use of words is crucial, actions still speak loudest (Prov 16:24; 20:11). They consistently think before they speak (Prov 29:20). They consistently say less than they think (Prov 29:11). They value work and self-control as highly as God does (Prov 16:32; 18:9; 25:28). They fear the deadly sin of pride (Prov 3:34; 14:15–16). The mature recognize that there are many things more valuable than money (Prov 22:1; 31:10; Matt 16:26). The mature live in biblical balance (Prov 23:4–5; 30:7–9).

DISCUSSION QUESTIONS

1. How is a "babe in Christ" different from a mature Christian? Compare and contrast these two believers.

2. Suggest a spiritual growth plan for Christian maturity. What actions or steps can be taken to grow toward maturity in Christ?

3. Does God urge every Christian to grow toward maturity?

4. In what ways does involvement in the work of ministry help Christians mature?

5. Why might some think the path to spiritual maturity includes adding manmade rules and requirements to God's plan?

6. What are the dangers of such additions?

7. According to Colossians 2, what are those who propose such additions implying about Jesus?

8. The final paragraph in this lesson heavily links maturity and wisdom. Is this linkage justified? How so?

ELEVEN
SPEAKING THE TRUTH IN LOVE

One of the beauties of Scripture is its balance. As a truth-loving, truth-teaching servant of the Lord, Paul noted the dangers of deception which being equipped for ministry would lead Christians to avoid (Eph 4:14). In the very next verse, the apostle reminds us how believers are to oppose deceptive doctrine. Knowing how to speak the truth in love is a vital aspect of being equipped for the work of ministry. Speaking the truth in love is evidence of Christian growth into the image of Christ.

BIBLICAL EXAMPLES

Christians are passionate about truth. We are zealous for Christ. But we know both passion and zeal must be tempered by knowledge and love. Luke 9:51–56 teaches this so clearly. A village of the Samaritans learned that Jesus was passing through on His way to Jerusalem. Because of the bitterness between the Samaritans and the Jews, the people of that village refused to show hospitality to Him. This insult incensed James and John.

In what they must have believed to be righteous indignation, the disciples said to Jesus, "Lord, do You want us to command fire to come down from heaven and consume them, just as Elijah did?" (Luke 9:54). They were standing up for Jesus. They were taking a stand. They were showing their faith.

Luke 9:54–55 read, "But He turned and rebuked them, and said, 'You do not know what manner of spirit you are of. For the Son of Man did not come to destroy men's lives but to save them.'" In their zeal to stand up for Jesus, they forgot the mission of Jesus. In their zeal to show their faith, they forgot the Christ-like attitude which should always accompany faith.

The Lord Himself spoke hard words when such words were needed. Matthew 23 makes this clear. But Matthew 23:37–39 clearly show that those words were spoken out of love. One reason that the Lord could speak with such clarity and power is that He knew men's hearts. In that we do not, our words must be measured carefully. The example of the archangel Michael helps remind us. Even when contending with the devil, that holy being "dared not bring against him a reviling accusation, but said, 'The Lord rebuke you!'" (Jude 9).

Paul spoke hard words when such words were needed. He bluntly confronted "preacheritis" in Corinth, but he did so pleading with them as brethren "by the name of our Lord Jesus Christ" (1 Cor 1:10). He commanded the church to deliver their immoral brother "to Satan for the destruction of the flesh," but with the motive "that his spirit may be saved in the day of the Lord Jesus" (1 Cor 5:5). Even as he chastised the brethren for their misuse of spiritual gifts, he reminded them of their unity in Christ (1 Cor 12). He reminded them of the "more excellent way," the way of love (1 Corinthians 12:31; 13:1–13).

Paul, when essential for the defense of the gospel, rebuked Peter "to his face" (Gal 2:11). But this rebuke carried no personal malice. We're confident that it met the inspired standard of Galatians 6:1–5. To the eternal credit of both men, it did not destroy their relationship (2 Pet 3:14–16). It stands as a powerful application of Proverbs 27:5–6 and 28:23.

Another strong example of speaking the truth in love is found in the parable of the prodigal son. Notice the way the father reasoned with his elder son. First, "his father came out and pleaded with him" (Luke 15:28). Though his son was in the wrong, the father made the first move. Then, he listened to his son's complaint. He knew that listening was important, and that listening does not imply agreement. Finally, he spoke lovingly to his son. Despite the son's venom, his father called him "son." He affirmed his relationship and commitment to his son (v. 31). He acknowledged the wrongdoing of the prodigal, "your brother was dead" (v. 32). And he acknowledged the boy's "rebirth," describing him as "alive again" (v. 32). What an engaging and powerful appeal!

Two outstanding Old Testament examples must be mentioned, both involving King David. 1 Samuel 25 records David's highly negative encounter with Nabal. After protecting Nabal's servants and flocks, David sent an envoy to request hospitality. Nabal responded with stinging rudeness (v. 10-11). Abigail, Nabal's wife, quickly learned of the insult. Examine her speech to David. It is the epitome of humility and honesty. Truth was told in a way that saved lives, if not souls.

The example from 2 Samuel 12 is just as challenging. David has sinned grievously against God, Uriah, Bathsheba, his family, and the nation. To this point the sin is somewhat hidden. There has been no repentance. Nathan used a divinely inspired parable to help David tell himself the truth about his sin. What an example of speaking the truth in love! God reached out to His king because God knew that he would repent.

A WORD ABOUT ANGER

Some mistakenly believe that all anger is sin. Clearly this is not the case (Eph 4:26–27). God's anger is well documented (Exod 4:14; Num 11:1, 10; Psa 7:6). Jesus was angry as He saw the hardness of men's hearts (Mark 3:5). Anger can be an appropriate and powerful emotion.

Trouble comes when anger gains control. God saw that beginning to happen to Cain (Gen 4:1–8). He urged Cain to examine the reason for his anger and to exercise self-control. The Lord's counsel is still sound. We have the ability to evaluate our emotions. No matter how strong an emotion may be, we have the God-given ability to choose righteous behavior. Righteous behavior includes righteous, loving words.

Anger tends to shut down higher thinking. It tends to make us forget that every human is made in the image of God. It tends to make us forget that we, too, have our moments of foolishness and sin. It takes spiritual wisdom to rightly employ the energy of anger. We know the conventional wisdom, "When angry count to ten. When very angry count to 100." Spiritual wisdom is stronger. When angry pray. When angry meditate on the truth of scripture. When angry revisit 1 Corinthians 13, Luke 23:34, and Acts 7:60.

Even in defense of the gospel, we must avoid the temptation to "enjoy a good fight." We think of elders as mature leaders and examples to the church. 1 Timothy 3:1–7 reminds us that elders must be "not violent ... but gentle, not quarrelsome." Titus 2:2 suggests that being sound in love and in patience are just as important as being sound in faith. 1 Corinthians 13 describes love as being patient and kind, as not being rude in behavior and as not being easily provoked. 2 Timothy 2:24–26 add, "And a servant of the Lord must not quarrel but be gentle to all, able to teach, patient, in humility correcting those who are in opposition, if God perhaps, will grant them repentance, so that they may know the truth, and that they may come to their senses, and escape the snare of the devil."

The source is lost to this writer and the "quotation" may be paraphrased, but the words are valuable: "Destroy your enemy. Utterly destroy your enemy. Permanently destroy your enemy. Make him your friend." Those words fit 1 Timothy 2:1–7. God "desires all men to be saved and to come to the knowledge of the truth" (v. 4). Therefore, He wills that we pray for all men and that we "lead a quiet and peaceable life in all godliness and reverence" (v. 2). Speaking the truth in love will help us lead such a life. It will help us "pursue peace with all" and avoid falling "short of the grace of God" (Heb 12:12–17).

Christians who are equipped for the work of ministry certainly stand for truth (1 Tim 1:3–4; Jude 3). But we take that stand gently, humbly, and patiently (1 Pet 3:13–17). We have that attitude because we have set apart [sanctified, recognized as holy] "the Lord God in our hearts." Even when standing up for God's truth, our goal is not merely to win the argument or to prove our point. Our goal is to lead others to love God and to faithfully follow Him.

"Speaking the truth in love" is an art. It is best studied by noting how Jesus spoke to people. The gospels are filled with outstanding examples. Like Nathan before David, Jesus used stories to teach without insulting and to make people think (Luke 7:36–50; 2 Sam 12). Jesus could turn His own need into a way to begin a spiritual conversation (John 4:1–26). He showed tremendous skill in helping the woman at the well want to know God's truth. Jesus masterfully used silence (John 8:1–12). He had remarkable ability in leading even His opponents to re-think their situation from a spiritual perspective. He was the master of the effective use of questions (Matt 21:23–32).

Colossians 4:5–6 offers direct instructions to Christians: "Walk in wisdom toward those who are outside, redeeming the time. Let your speech always be with grace, seasoned with salt, that you may know how you ought to answer each one."

This passage reminds us that "speaking the truth in love" is both an attitude and an art. It is learned only by prayerful, consistent practice. But when we learn it, people will recognize that we belong to Jesus.

SPEAKING THE TRUTH WITHOUT LOVE

What happens when Christians commit the sin of speaking the truth without love? Feelings are hurt. Barriers are erected. Errant positions are entrenched. Scripture is violated. And confusion reigns.

If people know nothing else about God, they know 1 John 4:8, "For God is love." Even if they don't yet appreciate the gift, they often know John 3:16, "For God so loved the world that He gave His only begotten Son, that whoever believes in Him should not perish but have everlasting life." Even if they don't know the citation, they know the truth of 1 John 4:7 and Matthew 5:44—Christians are supposed to love both their brethren and their enemies. When truth is spoken without love, crucial aspects of truth are denied. When truth is spoken without love, God is misrepresented. When truth is spoken without love, soul-saving opportunity is lost.

DISCUSSION QUESTIONS

1. In what situations do you find it most difficult to speak the truth in love?

2. What is the harm or loss if the truth is spoken, but not in love?

3. 1 Samuel 25 is a classic example of wise, effective communication. What can we learn from the way Abigail talked to David?

4. Would you be a Christian today if the first thing you ever heard about the Lord and His church had been presented to you in the tone and approach that you use with others (or have heard some use with others)?

5. As Matthew 21:23–32 shows, Jesus did not answer every question that was posed to Him. Why not? What can we learn from this example?

6. Is anger the primary reason that Christians sometimes speak the truth without love? Explain. What might be other reasons?

7. Revisit the section "Speaking the Truth Without Love." Is that section overstated or exaggerated? Explain.

TWELVE
EVERY PART DOING ITS SHARE

The apostle Paul loved to speak of the church as the body of Christ. We remember Ephesians 5:23b, "Christ is the head of the church; and He is the Savior of the body." In explaining the Lord's love for the church, Paul continues, "For we are members of His body, of His flesh, and of His bones" (Eph 5:30). Ephesians 4:25 says, "For we are members of one another." 1 Corinthians 12:13 offers dual proofs of our oneness in Christ, "For by one Spirit we were all baptized into one body—whether Jews or Greeks, whether slaves or free—and have all been made to drink into one Spirit."

Ephesians 4:11–16 reminds us that the Lord's body, His church, is living and growing. It grows in unity "by what every joint supplies." Its growth is caused, at least in part, by effective working as "every part does its share." We are wise to remember that even as every part does its part, "It is God who works in you both to will and to do His good pleasure (Phil 2:12–13). Paul offers a more detailed discussion of our working together for the good of the body in 1 Corinthians 12.

1 CORINTHIANS 12: HOW THE BODY WORKS

As with every part of Scripture, it is essential that we read 1 Corinthians 12 in context. 1 Corinthians 12–14 deal with miraculous spiritual gifts as used and misused by the Corinthian Christians. We have previously acknowledged that the age of those miraculous gifts has passed. It ended shortly after the time of the apostles. That being true, vital and lasting principles are taught in 1 Corinthians 12, principles which tell us much about how the body of Christ works.

In the age of miraculous spiritual gifts, not every believer had the same gift. Paul acknowledges, "There are differences of ministries, but the same Lord. There are differences of activities, but it is the same God who works in all" (1 Cor 12:5–6). Similarly, not every believer has the same aptitudes and abilities today. Any gifts that we possess come from God. Whatever gifts we possess, we have due to God's will and grace. "But now God has set the members, each one of them, in the body just as He pleased" (1 Cor 12:18). There is strength and benefit in the diversity and distribution of gifts.

Whatever each believer's gift might be, "The manifestation of the Spirit is given to each one for the profit of all" (1 Cor 12:7). No gift of God is intended to be used selfishly. Each talent and ability is meant to serve, encourage, and strengthen the body (1 Cor 14:12ff). We are blessed so that we can be a blessing. Our focus is never, "Look at me! Notice how special

God has made me." Rather our focus is, "Thank God for giving me opportunity to serve! How can I best help my
brethren?"

Even though it has many members, the body is one (1 Cor
12:12–14). Because the body has many members, attention
must be given to maintaining unity (Eph 4:1–6). Whether in
the age of miracles or today, "There are diversities of gifts,
but the same Spirit. There are diversities of ministries, but
the same Lord. And there are diversities of activities, but it
is the same God who works all in all" (1 Cor 12:4–6). The
body is united under its one Head.

Different parts of the body have different functions (1 Cor
12:15–21). Each function and each part are important. No
argument is made that each function is equally important, but
each part is a precious soul that is worth more than all the
world. The body functions as its various members (parts) each
perform their respective functions. If any part is missing or
any part fails, the body suffers harm.

The parts of the body that are considered weaker are still
necessary (1 Cor 12:22). In fact, those parts of the body may
need the greatest care (1 Cor 12:22–25). Every member matters—always (Eph 4:16).

The body takes care of itself. "And if one member suffers,
all the members suffer with it; or if one member is honored,
all the members rejoice with it" (1 Cor 12:26). For full health,
each member of the body must be well. For full effectiveness,
each part of the body must do its share.

IMPLICATIONS FOR BELIEVERS TODAY

We need one another. That is one reason the Lord adds the saved to the church (Acts 2:47). We need one another's encouragement. A coal separated from the fire quickly becomes cold. Leave it with the others, and its heat is maintained. A team can support the members who get "down" (Eccles 4:9–12). When we're alone, it's so much easier for discouragement to overcome us. That's what happened to Elijah following the stunning victory on Mount Carmel. In explaining his despair to God, Elijah said, they have "killed Your prophets with the sword. I alone am left; and they seek to take my life" (1 Kgs 19:14). Part of God's cure for Elijah's despair was having Elisha work with him. Another part was informing him that seven thousand others also remained faithful (1 Kgs 19:16–18).

Every part of the body has a share in the work of ministry. The church is not a body where only "the experts" are qualified to contribute. Many religious groups recognize a professional clergy. We reject this concept as unbiblical. However, we know that it is difficult to avoid thinking like the culture around us. Some tend to think of "The Minister" as the expert, the only one truly qualified to minister. Others may think of him as the man we pay to do our ministry for us. We must work to countermand this unbiblical view. "Minister" merely means servant. "Ministry" is service. We cannot imitate our Lord without being ministers (Matt 20:28).

"BY WHICH EVERY PART DOES ITS SHARE"

The phrase above is from Ephesians 4:16. Rightly understood and applied, it is a sound and biblical concept. Wrongly applied or misunderstood, it becomes both dangerous and divisive. The devil stands ready to help us misunderstand.

Some view this phrase critically, as permission or even encouragement to evaluate the respective contributions of their fellow Christians. Our brothers and sisters are labeled as "doing their share," "doing less than they could," or "not doing their share." We are wise and biblical to "consider one another in order to stir up love and good works" (Heb 10:25). This series of lessons has continually encouraged a proactive stance toward involving others in God's service. However, Scripture has nothing good to say about the judgmental stance of "rating" the service of others. 2 Corinthians 10:12 speaks of such people, saying, "But they, measuring themselves by themselves, and comparing themselves among themselves, are not wise."

Some view this phrase apologetically, as excuse for limited service. "You know me. I'm just a one talent man. If life were different, if I didn't have all these obligations and limitations, I could really do something for the Lord." While Moses lived and died long before the letter to the Ephesians was penned, he attempted to explain his limitations to God. God's rebuke in Exodus 4:11 is clear. Exodus 4:14 adds, "So the anger of the Lord was kindled against Moses." God does not take a positive view of excuses.

Some view this phrase demandingly, seeking ever increasing help from others to "meet my needs." While Scripture is absolutely clear that Christians help one another (Gal 6:10; Phil 2:3–4), it never promotes the concept of demanding service from the brethren (Rom 12:3–21). To paraphrase a president, "Ask not what your brethren can do for you. Ask what you can do for your brethren." The emphasis must be on serving rather than on being served.

Some view this phrase hopelessly. "No matter how much I do for Jesus, it will never be enough. I can never pay the debt that I owe." Some link James 4:17, "Therefore, to him who knows to do good and does not do it, to him it is sin." They emphasize the fact that no one serves God perfectly, that one seldom—if ever—literally does all good that he knows to do. We would never speak a word against doing God's will (Matt 7:21–27; John 14:15; 15:14). However, we know that our good deeds cannot save us (Eph 2:8–9). Rather, we "walk" in good works because "we are His workmanship, created in good works, which God prepared beforehand that we should walk in them" (Eph 2:10).

We are wise to view this phrase personally. Am I doing what I should? Am I using the abilities that God has given me? Am I seizing the opportunities that God puts before me? Am I growing in service to the body? Am I making serious effort to grow?

We are wise to view this phrase encouragingly. By the grace of God, I can contribute to the growth of the body. By the grace of God, I have something to offer. My gift, no matter how small, can be multiplied by God. Like those described in

3 John 8, we can become "fellow workers for the truth." Just as Paul and Apollos were "God's fellow workers" (1 Cor 3:9), we are greatly honored to have opportunity to serve.

We are wise to view this phrase as a challenge. No matter how much we are blessed to serve, God can bring us to greater heights of service (Matt 25:21). No matter how much we have done, "there is much to do, there's work on every hand." We have not yet come "to the measure of the stature of the fullness of Christ." (Eph 4:13).

The Lord's work is big enough to need every single worker. Even little toes and fingernails have a role to fulfill. When it comes to the well-being of the body, every contribution counts. We may be tempted to think, "The little that I can do really doesn't matter." Ephesians 4:16 disagrees. The little boy with the loaves and fish didn't feed the 5,000, but his part mattered (John 6:1–14). The widow's two coins had very little value, but they mattered to Jesus (Mark 12:41–44). From a worldly point of view, the entire church in Smyrna seemed persecuted and poor. Jesus called them rich and promised them the crown of life (Rev 2:8–11). We dare not underestimate the power of faithfulness. We never know the power of even the smallest good deed. Whatever the specific work of ministry, it becomes great when it is done to the glory of God.

DISCUSSION QUESTIONS

1. Is it true that every Christian has a meaningful share in God's work of ministry? How do we know?

2. Why do many Christians seem to find that hard to believe? How would it help every Christian to believe this truth?

3. How do I know if I am doing my part in the work of ministry?

4. How can the phrase "my share in the work" be misunderstood?

5. Does the absence of miraculous gifts make us less equipped for ministry today?

6. Why do some find it easier to judge the work and commitment of others than to evaluate their own Christian service?

7. Why do some find it so easy to underestimate the power and blessing of even the smallest Christian service?

THIRTEEN
CAUSING GROWTH OF THE BODY

When spiritual leaders equip members of the body for the work of ministry, the church will grow in love, in unity, in Christ-likeness, in stability, in maturity, and in encouragement. If the church is growing in all these ways, it is hard to imagine that it could be kept from also growing in number. This is true for many reasons.

CATEGORIES OF CHURCH GROWTH

Ephesians 4:11-16 emphasizes the equipping, edifying, maturing, ministry, and function of the church. This emphasis invites us to think more broadly about church growth. The church grows as the saints are equipped. The church grows as the body is edified. The church grows as the saints mature into the image of Christ. The church grows as doctrinal stability is enhanced. The church grows when every member learns to speak the truth in love. The church grows as each member steps up to his or her role in God's work.

The paragraph above is in no way intended to diminish purposeful, direct evangelism. In no way does it negate the commissions of Matthew 28:18–20 and Mark 16:15–16 or the admonition to pray in Matthew 9:38. The gospel "is the power of God to salvation for everyone who believes" (Rom 1:16). "It pleased God through the foolishness of the message preached to save those who believe" (1 Cor 1:21). But the message is never preached in a vacuum. The gospel is preached most effectively in the context of a faithful, loving, and vibrant church. Ephesians 4:11–16 describes such a church.

God's Plan for Growth

Ephesians 4 describes leaders who will attract good people. Equipping leaders—those who work to equip the saints—are nothing like the despotic worldly leaders whom Jesus described in Matthew 20:25–28. They shepherd the flock, following the example of The Good Shepherd (John 10:1–30). They serve as leaders, not as lords (1 Pet 5:1–4). Because they lead like Jesus and for Jesus, they reflect the beauty of Jesus.

Ephesians 4 describes leaders and churches (congregations) who help produce healthy Christians. We rightly stress the importance of the new birth (John 3:1–21). We count it a joy whenever anyone dies with Christ through repentance, is buried with Christ through baptism, and rises to newness of life in Christ (Rom 6; Gal 3:26–29; Col 2:11–14). But we also rightly recognize baptism as the beginning of a new life.

Paul describes this new life as a putting "on the new man which was created according to God in true righteousness and holiness" (Eph 4:24). It is an ongoing imitation of Jesus (Matt 10:24–25a; 1 Cor 11:1). It involves a new way of thinking and a new way of living (Rom 12:1–2; Eph 4:17–24). Just as Jesus "went about doing good," so do His disciples (Acts 10:38). Just as Jesus committed His life to God's service, so do His disciples (Matt 20:28). An equipping church honors Jesus as it helps people become more like Him.

Ephesians 4 describes happy, healthy Christians. Involved, active Christians know the joy of serving God. They have a purpose and a mission. Involved, active Christians continue to grow in knowledge, faith, and love. Such disciples are easy to notice. They have something that the people want, something that attracts people. And when people do take notice, they can be taught the good news of Jesus Christ.

Ephesians 4 describes a church where every member is respected and valued. The leaders believe and teach that every believer can be equipped for the work of ministry. Every member is needed. Teamwork and mutual support abound.

Ephesians 4 describes a united church. It is united in its love for God and its commitment to His truth. Its unity is continually growing stronger. There is one Lord, one faith, one body, and one cause.

THE BLESSINGS OF GROWTH

1 Corinthians 3:6 documents the fact that God is the power behind church growth. However, the previous verse

acknowledges that God gives faithful ministers the blessing of assisting that growth. Ephesians 4:11–16 establishes the truth that every Christian is called to be a faithful minister.

Biblical growth begets growth. It creates a blessed cycle of expectation, evangelism, and enthusiasm. We see that cycle in the early chapters of Acts. We see it again in Acts 11:19–26 in Antioch. Disciples with vision, faith, and big hearts preached the Lord Jesus to everyone without ethnic distinction. These disciples are not named within Scripture. Could this be God's way of emphasizing the grassroots nature of their evangelistic work? Could this be the Lord's way of reminding us that this is the normal condition of His church? "And the hand of the Lord was with them, and a great number believed and turned to the Lord" (v. 21). Barnabas recognized this as the presence of the grace of God. Not only did he encourage them "to keep on keeping on," he made the journey to Tarsus to add Saul to this great gospel work. We're not at all surprised that the Holy Spirit called His first formal mission team from this congregation (Acts 13:1–3).

Acts 11:19–26 exude positive energy. The good news of many conversions could not be contained within Antioch. The church in Jerusalem took notice. It is our conviction that other congregations also took notice and were encouraged. We cannot be certain whether the name "Christian" originated inside or outside the church, but we believe it to be direct fulfillment of Isaiah 62:2. We believe it a great honor that God let the disciples first be called Christians in Antioch.

While the Lord is our ultimate example, His people need the ongoing encouragement of exemplary congregations. No congregation will be perfect; mere humans don't reach that lofty goal in this life. However, even imperfection cannot rob a congregation of the opportunity to encourage others. Like Antioch, Rome, Macedonia, and Thessalonica, we can be bright lights to our brethren (Acts 11; Rom 1:8; 2 Cor 8; 1 Thess 1:6–8).

THE CHALLENGES OF GROWTH

Along with tons of blessings, church growth also brings challenges. This has been true from the first days of the church. There were physical needs to be met (Acts 2:45; 4:34–35; 6:1–7). There was persecution (Acts 4:1–22; 5:17–42; 7:54–8:3). There were disciples who fell into sin (Acts 5:1–11). There were complaints of favoritism in ministry (Acts 6:1–7). There was a need to add additional leadership and structure to the work (Acts 6:1–7). There were doctrinal issues that threatened the faithfulness and unity of the church (Acts 15).

Growth always brings change, and change can be scary. Ephesians 4:11–16 offers keys to keeping that change positive and biblical. God-ordained leaders recognize and embrace their roles as equippers of the saints. The saints don't think of themselves as "just ordinary Christians." They view themselves as the redeemed, as those empowered by God for ministry. No one asks, "What's in this for me? How can this church meet my needs?" The mindset is, "How can I help? What can I do to bless my brethren?" People aren't satisfied with "just keeping house" or "maintaining." They take to heart the biblical challenges to edify the body, to grow in unity, to maintain doctrinal soundness, and to increase in knowledge of Jesus and our imitation of Him. They seek the stability that only truth can bring. They seek the joy of genuine, biblical, every-member ministry.

WHAT DO WE DO NOW?

Good people want Jesus' church to grow. Good people want to love the Lord and to give their best to Him. Good people want to live up to the truth of Scripture. But, what do we do if we find ourselves or the congregation where we worship falling short of the truth taught in Ephesians 4:1–16?

This series of lessons was written in support of revival. Spiritual revival can begin anywhere and anytime that a Christian humbles himself before God. What can we do now?

- We assess. We look at our lives in the mirror of the Word. We face the truth (2 Cor 13:5). We invite God to help us face the truth (Psa 139:23–24).
- We repent. We confess our sins to God and pray for His forgiveness (Psa 51:3–4, 10–13).
- We pray. We pray for God's wisdom, guidance, and blessing (Jam 1:5–6).
- We begin. Whatever we need to do to step up to God's calling, we do. We commit ourselves to becoming better equipped for the work of ministry. As we work to become equipped for His service,

we also work to equip others (1 Sam 1:9; Isa 6:8–9).

- We persevere. We never let this process stop (Col 3:23, 24; 2 Tim 4:7–8).

God still blesses His people with growth. God still blesses His church with growth. As individual Christians grow, the body is moved to grow. We know that, in a sense, each one is only one. But we also know better. We know that each Christian is never just one. We live in Christ, for Christ, and with Christ.

DISCUSSION QUESTIONS

1. Given the ever-worsening world in which we live, is church growth still possible? Explain your answer.

2. We have described Ephesians 4 in terms which some have called "a church growth atmosphere." Do you believe such an atmosphere actually encourages people to want to hear the gospel? Explain.

3. What leads equipping leaders—those who labor to equip others for the work of ministry—to do that challenging and difficult work? What keeps them motivated? How will taking "an equipping stance"—working to equip every Christian for the work of ministry—affect the influence of church leaders? How will failing to take such a "stance" affect the church?

What barriers might hinder leaders from taking "an equipping stance"?

4. Can one person really make a difference in the growth of a congregation? Explain.

5. Is it biblical to describe church growth in the broad terms used above? Explain. What are potential dangers of using such broad terms? What are the potential dangers of failing to see church growth as broadly as the Bible describes it?

6. What will you do to encourage the growth of the body today?

INDEX OF SCRIPTURE REFERENCES